Winning the Battle

OVER NEGATIVE EMOTIONS

Dr. Kerwin B. Lee

To Anne,
Keep all Your
dreams alive!,

Kerwin Lee

Exody
14:14

Orman Press
Lithonia, Georgia

Winning the Battle
OVER NEGATIVE EMOTIONS

by
Dr. Kerwin B. Lee

Copyright © 2003
A Word for the Times Ministries

ISBN: 1-891773-46-1

Scripture quotations are taken from THE HOLY BIBLE, *King James Version,* or are the author's paraphrase of that version.

Printed in the United States of America

9 8 7 6 5 4 3 2

Publishing Services Provided By
Orman Press, Inc.
Lithonia, Georgia

— *Dedication* —

To my bayou beauty, my wife, Yolanda, for accepting my marriage proposal, being the best spouse there is for me and for turning our house into a home.

• • • • • •

To my father, Philip Lee, for your insistence that I go to the library and ensuring that I only read challenging material.

• • • • • •

To my mother, Thelma Lee, for showing me by your example, encouragement and endurance that negative emotions can be overcome.

• • • • • •

To my second mother, Relia Lee, for keeping the dream that God gave you about my doing great things ever before me.

— *Acknowledgements* —

To God, for saving me, sustaining me and speaking to me about this book.

To my baby, my wife, Yolanda, for your support of my ministry, the strength you bring to our marriage and the way you share me with multitudes.

To my legacy, my sons, Kerwin II and Kernard, for the inspiration that you bring to me and the many preaching and teaching illustrations you provide. Hallelujah!

To my brothers, Keith, Kevin and Kincaid for all the fun we had growing up and the fellowship we have today.

To the sister that I never had, Brenda Moore, thanks for the friendship, fellowship and relationship that we share.

To the people I'm privileged to pastor, Berean Christian Church. Thanks for your unconditional love, labor and liberality.

To my administrative assistant, Peggy Walker, for believing and seeing where God was taking me long ago.

To my editor, Andrea Mitchell, for your eyes, expertise, and excellence. Thanks for helping me to understand the difference between preaching and writing.

Last but not least, to believers everywhere who have encouraged, equipped and educated me.

— *Table of Contents* —

Winning The Battle Over
NEGATIVE EMOTIONS

One of the highlights of Jesus' earthly ministry is recorded in Matthew 3:17. The event is the baptism of Jesus and the highlight is God saying Jesus is His beloved son and in Him, God is well pleased. I am sure this public declaration by God had to make Jesus feel good.

For the past seventeen years, I have had the blessed privilege to be the spiritual father and pastor of Dr. Kerwin B. Lee. I would like to echo about my spiritual son, Kerwin, what God said about His son, Jesus. He is my beloved son and in him I am well pleased.

I have watched him grow as an individual, minister and a pastor. His first book release, *Winning the Battle Over Negative Emotions*, is yet another tangible example of his diversity and growth. It has been a joy as his spiritual mentor to be a part of what God is certainly doing in his life.

It is often said, "Winning isn't everything." However, in order to survive spiritually, it is imperative that you win the battle over your negative emotions. This is why Dr. Lee's book, *Winning the Battle Over Negative Emotions*, would be an asset to your Christian library.

In his book, Dr. Lee examines eight common emotions that keep us from our spiritual freedom. Using actual biblical characters, he not only shows that these emotions can happen to anyone, but shares practical ways to overcome them.

I highly recommend this book to everyone because all of us, at some point, have had a difficult time dealing with a negative emotion. It is my prayer that this book will be used as a tool to help individuals overcome bitterness, depression, fear, grief, guilt, hatred, jealousy and worry.

Bishop James H. Morton
Senior Pastor
New Beginnings Full Gospel Baptist Church
Decatur, Georgia

Winning The Battle Over
NEGATIVE EMOTIONS

W hat are negative emotions? Jealousy, grief, worry, hatred, guilt, depression, bitterness, anxiety—the list goes on and on. What causes them to surface? It is amazing that these negative emotions and feelings we experience have all been experienced by biblical characters. This suggests that if it happened to people in the Bible, it can happen to anyone.

Although we have biblical role models who experienced and overcame these emotions, many Christians still do not understand that it is possible to go to church and still experience negative emotions. Not only is it possible to go to church and experience these feelings, it is also possible to love the Lord and experience them.

Everyone is emotional because everyone has emotions. The word "emotion" is defined as a strong feeling. There is nothing wrong with having strong feelings as long as those feelings are not negative and do not control you. Negative emotions that control you are not only dangerous, but they can also be destructive.

The biblical people who struggled with these emotions were people who were strong in the Lord. It is important to remember this fact because if you are not careful, you might think you could reach a level with God where you are immune to such circumstances. However, that is not the case. Most people who think they are immune are really in denial.

Perhaps the most important question is not related to the definition of negative emotions, but rather, "How do I overcome negative emotions?"

This book spotlights eight negative emotions experienced by different people in the Bible. Through an examination of these godly people and relevant Scriptures, you will learn what causes negative emotions and, most importantly, how to overcome them.

CHAPTER ONE

Winning The Battle Over
BITTERNESS

— I Samuel 1 —

The prophet Samuel was born out of a bitter and prayerful struggle by his mother, Hannah. First Samuel 1:10 says, *"And she was in bitterness of soul and prayed unto the Lord and wept sore."* Hannah is the main character of the first chapter of I Samuel. The first nine verses reveal what drove her soul to bitterness. Hannah was burdened because she was unable to have a child.

Meanwhile, Peninnah, her husband's other wife, kept having children. Elkanah loved Hannah more, so Peninnah's way of getting even was to have more babies and torment Hannah about her barrenness. The Bible says the Lord closed Hannah's womb. In those days, a woman who did not have a child was viewed as being less than a woman. Hannah's barrenness was her burden and it made her home miserable because of the other wife, Peninnah.

In the latter part of Chapter 1, you see Hannah giving birth. Hannah's experience suggests that many times birth follows burdens. Sometimes God will allow you to become burdened because He is getting ready to birth something

If you are involved with people, there is a good chance that bitterness is going to creep in somehow.

that you could not do on your own. After the burden and the birth, you see the blessing throughout the rest of the Book of I Samuel. Hannah's son, Samuel, became a blessing for many people. Often, on our spiritual journey there is the burden, the birth and then the blessing. If what you are birthing is not turning into a blessing, it may not be a pregnancy by God. When God gives you something or someone, it will always turn into a blessing.

When reading I Samuel 1:1–9, you will discover that bitterness is personal. It is not something that happens only to your boss, neighbor or your friends. It can happen to you, too.

Not only can bitterness be personal, it can also be relational. Hannah was bitter because of her relationship with her husband's other wife, Penninah. If you are involved with people, there is a good chance that bitterness will creep in somehow. If you are dealing with people in any way at all, some bitterness will occur.

Bitterness is not only personal and relational, it can also be residential. That is, it can reside in your home. First Samuel 1:6 tells how Penninah agitated Hannah, got on her nerves, frustrated her and caused residential bitterness. Residential bitterness is just another expression for a living hell on earth.

If that were not enough, Hannah also found herself experiencing physical bitterness. First Samuel 1:7 tells us that Hannah lost her appetite, which probably means she lost weight. The strain of her bitterness began to show on her body and moved her to tears because of her barreness and the treatment she received from Peninnah.

Finally, verse 8 reveals that Hannah was affected emotionally by her bitterness. No matter who you are or what physical features you have, if you have a relationship with people, you are a candidate for bitterness. You are a candidate for bitterness because there is an emotional side to everyone. Hannah experienced bitterness personally, relationally, residentially, physically and emotionally, but she got over it!

Overcoming Bitterness

No matter what the problem or how long it has been going on, you can overcome bitterness. It does not matter who caused the problem or why; you can get over it. Stop talking about why it happened and start looking at what you can do about it. I want to share five steps to overcoming bitterness based on Hannah's experience with overcoming her various kinds of bitterness.

1. Travel to God's House Locally

Although Hannah was not feeling well, she still went to church. Verse 7 tells us "...*she went up to the house of the Lord.*" She was not feeling well, but she still went to church. She was frustrated because things were not going her way, but she still went to church. Hannah knew her situation would not get better by sitting at home. Bitterness and frustration never get better while you are sitting at home. Being at home usually does not make the situation any smoother.

What destroys some of us today is that we do not spend enough time in church.

What destroys some of us today is that we do not spend enough time in church. Many of us are hindered from overcoming life's problems because we do not have a local church home. We go to church nationally via television and radio, but will not attend a church in our community. Some of us are still talking about the church we left—but we live in another state!

2. Turn to God Quickly

Although Hannah was bitter, I Samuel 1:10 says that she also prayed. As soon as you begin to feel bitter, get on your knees and turn to God. As soon as you feel like taking your bitterness out on someone or lashing out at someone in anger, you have to pray. When feelings of bitterness swell up inside of you, turn to God quickly. Taking too much time between when you get bitter and when you start praying will hinder you from overcoming it.

3. Talk to God Honestly

Hannah began talking to God in verse 11. She said, *"Remember me" (I Sam. 1:11).* She had problems at home with her husband and his other wife, but when she prayed, she dealt with her issue. She did not tell God to fix everybody else. She asked God to fix her. Hannah was able to focus on the main problem. She told God, "What I really need is a child. That's my real problem."

Hannah was honest with God. Some of you have been praying to God, but you have not been honest with Him. You told God to move your supervisor out of the way, but your supervisor has nothing to do with your getting to work late. If there is anyone with whom you can be honest, it is God. You can tell Him just how you feel. You do not have to worry about hurting God's feelings. He can take it however you dump it. Tell God the truth about your needs.

4. Trust God Completely

Hannah asked God to give her a son. When she started praying, she was grieved, saddened and could not eat. Hannah was messed up. By the end of verse 18, Hannah was eating again and no longer sad. Hannah prayed for a child and although she was not pregnant when she left the temple, something was different. She was not sad anymore. Her circumstances had not changed, but she had.

Hannah's story suggests that before your circumstances change, you must change. Before your prayer is answered, you need to act like the answer is coming. If you have been asking God for a spouse, quit running around like you are single. Hannah realized that the way to move God is by doing what you can while He does what you cannot. Hannah recognized "I can't get myself pregnant, but I can change my attitude. I can't make this woman stop talking about me, but I can start eating." What hurts many of us is that we do not participate with God. We want to pray, but we do not want to work.

The Bible says that Hannah went her way and was no longer sad. That means that sometimes you have to turn it over to God and stop worrying about it. Give it to God and leave it alone.

5. Treat God's People Correctly

Hannah knew that in order to get what she wanted from God, she had to do more than just pray. She had to treat other people right. Do you remember when she was in the church praying? The Bible says that her lips were moving, but she was not making any sound. In I Samuel 1:14, Eli, the priest, came in and accused her of being drunk. He made a negative assumption without checking the facts.

It is easy to form a negative opinion when we see something we do not understand. Too many people in the church make negative assumptions. When we see something that we do not understand, sometimes the easiest thing to do is to form a negative opinion.

In verse 15, Hannah explained to Eli, "Lord, I'm not drunk." Although Eli disrespected her, she still respected him. A lot of saints would not have responded the way Hannah did. They would have told Eli off, regardless of the fact that he was a priest.

Why was Hannah able to be respectful to Eli? When you need something from God, you cannot allow people to pull you down to their level. You have to pull them up to your level. You cannot let anyone or anything—demon, devil, man or woman—stop you from receiving what you want from God. When you need a miracle, you do not have time to mistreat or disrespect others. When you need a blessing, you have to live higher than your enemy. You have to live higher than criticism and higher than the people who do not like you.

Because she treated Eli right and respected his position as a priest in the temple, he apologized to her. Imagine what might have

When we see something that we do not understand, sometimes the easiest thing to do is to form a negative opinion.

happened if Hannah had responded indignantly. You have to know when to be cool.

Verse 19 says, *"Elkanah knew Hannah his wife."* When Hannah returned home, she and her husband came together intimately. She had treated the preacher right at church, and then she came home and treated her husband right. Some of you may treat people right at church, but you are not doing the same thing at home.

When God shows up, He shows out.

Hannah slept with her husband because she knew that God works through people. She knew she could not receive from God if she did not trust Him. Trusting in God meant she had to put her negative feelings behind her and let God do what He wanted to do. After she was intimate with her husband, *"the Lord remembered her"* (I Sam. 1:19) and gave her a son.

When God shows up, He shows out. He showed up at the Red Sea and He showed out by parting the waters. He showed up at the Jordan River and He showed out by holding back the river's water. He showed up at the wall of Jericho and He showed out by making the walls tumble down. He showed up in the fiery furnace and He showed out by taking the heat out of the fire. He showed up in the lion's den and He showed out by making the lions go to sleep. He showed up in a Philippian jail and He showed out by opening the iron gates. He showed up on a hill called Calvary and He showed out by getting up early that Sunday morning with all power in His hands.

If He has not shown up for you, maybe it is because you do not have a local church home. Maybe He has not shown up because you will not turn to Him quickly. Maybe He has not shown up because you do not talk to Him openly and honestly. Maybe he has not shown up because you do not trust Him completely. Maybe He has not shown up because of the way you treat others. You need to let people know, "You're not important enough for me to hate you."

In I Samuel, Chapter 2, God gives Hannah five more children. She asked for one baby, but she got six. Eli, the priest who accused her of being drunk, raised Samuel. The same man who called her drunk trained her son for ministry.

If you had been in Hannah's place, would your memory have been too long to forgive Eli? Are you still talking about what happened in 1974? Drop that bitterness! It is hindering you. It will cause you to lose sleep and your friends.

Many times, the person with whom you are angry does not even know that you are mad. The same people who you allow to make your life miserable will be at your funeral because you let them kill you. Let them know you are bigger than that. What others mean for evil, God means for good. Remember, while someone is trying to break you, God is trying to make you. While someone is trying to mess you up, God is trying to bless you up. Trust God. He can touch your heart in ways no one else can.

CHAPTER TWO

Winning The Battle Over
DEPRESSION

— I Kings 19 —

lijah was a great prophet of God. Through him, God delivered a message of repentance and warning to His people. However, in I Kings 19, we discover that Elijah has fallen into a serious state of depression. No one is immune to depression, not even great men of God like Job, Gideon and King David. Although David was a man after God's own heart, he dealt with depression. Saul was so depressed that he went to a psychic for help. Jeremiah was so deeply depressed that he wanted to resign and give up on God and His people.

Ironically, Elijah's descent into depression came after one of the greatest events in his life, which was also one of the greatest events in biblical history. I Kings, Chapters 17 and 18, give you a true picture of the context of Chapter 19. In Chapter 17, you will discover Elijah's summons. In Chapter 18, you see Elijah's success, and in Chapter 19, you learn of Elijah's sorrow. He moved from being summoned, to being successful, to becoming sorrowful.

The reigning queen, the infamous Jezebel, imported 450 prophets from Baal into Israel. Elijah challenged and defeated them in Chapter 18. In the opening verse of Chapter 19, King Ahab told his wife what Elijah had done and she was furious. *"And Ahab told Jezebel all that Elijah had done, and withal how he had slain all the prophets with the sword."* This did not sit well with Jezebel, so she sent out a messenger with a death threat to Elijah: *"So let the gods do to me, and more also, if I make not thy life as the life of one of them by tomorrow about this time"* *(I Kings 19:2).* When Elijah heard the threat, he ran for his life and went to Beersheba, some twenty miles away.

Elijah stood up to 450 prophets boldly, but one woman put him on the run! He heard Jezebel's messenger say, "You're going to be dead by this time tomorrow." He believed and envisioned he would die, based on what he heard. I am suggesting that depression can set in when you internalize and visualize things you hear. Elijah ran until he came to Beersheba, which belonged to Judah, and left his servant there. He ran so fast that he left his servant. The servant's job was to help, support and encourage him, but Elijah left him behind.

First Kings 19:4 tells us that Elijah went on a day's journey into the wilderness, sat down under a juniper tree, and asked God to take his life: *"It is enough; now, O Lord, take away my life; for I am not better than my fathers."*

At this point, Elijah had fallen into depression. He had already gone a day's journey and not even thought about the fact that he was still alive. Despite Jezebel's threats, God kept him alive.

First Kings 19:5 says:

> *"And as he lay and slept under a juniper tree, behold then an angel touched him and said unto him, Arise and eat."*

Verse 6 tells us:

> *"And he looked, and, behold, there was a cake baked on the coals, and a cruse of water at his head. And he did eat and drink, and laid him down again."*

The brother ate and laid right back down! Verse 7 says:

> *"And the angel of the Lord came again the second time, and touched him, and said, Arise and eat; because the journey is too great for thee."*

The angel wanted Elijah to see that God still had work for him to do.

The angel wanted Elijah to see that God still had work for Him to do. The phrase *"Arise and eat, the journey is too great for you,"* (I Kings 19:7) means that there was work for Elijah to do. So Elijah ate and drank so he would have the strength to travel forty days and forty nights to Horeb, the mountain of God. At Horeb, God found him in a cave, scared and depressed, and asked him, "What are you doing here, Elijah?" (1 King 19:9).

The fact that the angel asked, "Why are you here?" suggests that it was not God's will for Elijah to be there. When you are some place you have no business being, God will ask "Why are you here?" If you go to the bar at happy hour, God will ask, "Why are you here?" If you are dating someone who does not believe in God, God will ask, "Why are you here?"

Elijah told the Lord, "I have been very zealous for You, Lord. The Israelites have rejected your covenant, broken down your altars, and put your prophets to death. I'm the only one left, and now they are trying to kill me, too" (I Kings 19:10). The Lord told Elijah to go and stand on the mountain where he would be in God's presence. The Lord promised to visit him there. The Bible tells us that a great and powerful wind tore the mountains apart and shattered the rocks, but the Lord was not in the wind. After the wind, there was an earthquake, but the Lord was not in the earthquake. After

When you are some place you have no business being, God will ask, "Why are you here?"

the earthquake there was a fire, but the Lord was not in the fire. After the fire, there was a still, small voice. When Elijah heard the voice, he wrapped his face in his mantle and stood at the cave's entrance. The voice said, "What are you doing here, Elijah?" The prophet repeated what he told the Lord in verse 10. Instead of responding to Elijah's fears and complaints, the Lord told him, "I want you to go anoint three people" (I Kings 19:15–16).

Do you see signs of depression here? Elijah was living on the run. He had isolated himself and was not eating. He went from the wilderness to the cave. He did not want to be around other people. He was low on energy, low on self-esteem, and suicidal.

What led to Elijah's depression? A few factors can be named. These conditions should be noted because if a great prophet of God like Elijah can experience depression, then so can anyone.

What Causes Depression?

It is important to know what leads you to depression. It is equally important to know ways to overcome depression. Let us look first at the causes of depression.

1. Fear

It is obvious that Elijah was afraid for his life (I King 19:3). Fear can cause you to be paranoid and blow a situation out of proportion. Elijah greatly exaggerated his circumstances because he was afraid. Elijah let one woman's threat make him forget his God had the power to call down fire from heaven. Fear can lead to depression.

2. Foes

Church members, co-workers, companions, children—anyone with whom you have a relationship can plunge you into deep depression, especially your enemies. Everyone has enemies. No matter how great you are, how beautiful you are or how well you treat people, you will have enemies. If Jesus had them, and he was perfect, you will have them, too. Elijah's enemies had threatened to kill him. Your foes can cause depression.

3. Fatigue

What caused Elijah to be tired? Some people actually run themselves into depression. People run from one church to another. Women run from one man to another. Men run from one woman to another. Some people run from one job, one city or one house to another. All of that running can lead to fatigue and depression.

4. Frustration

It is obvious that Elijah was frustrated because he asked God to take his life. He was

No matter how great you are, how beautiful you are or how well you treat people, you will have enemies.

suicidal. He had insecurities. His self-esteem was at an all-time low. Be careful to not let people, your job or everyday occurrences of life frustrate you. Do not let things that really do not matter frustrate you because frustration can lead to depression.

5. Failures

Elijah had just slaughtered all of Ahab and Jezebel's prophets. He hoped that the royal couple would turn their lives around as a result of what God had done through him. When Ahab and Jezebel did not change after seeing Elijah's power and anointing, he probably thought, "I've failed."

Sometimes parents fall into depression when their children go through negative circumstances. The devil tells them, "You've failed." When your teenage child gets pregnant, the devil says, "You've failed." When you are working hard on the job and get passed over for a promotion, the devil creeps into your mind and says, "You've failed." What about when your relationships do not work out? You work hard to keep yourself attractive. You are a good person, fun to be with and hard working, but one day, the person you love says, "I don't want you anymore." You are attractive, God-loving, fun-loving and financially secure, but that one person's rejection can make you think there is something wrong with you. The failures of life can pull us into a pit of depression.

6. Fruitfulness

God worked a miracle through Elijah in I Kings, Chapter 18. God has blessed most of us to experience great levels of success in life. You need to be careful when you are on the mountaintop of success. Some people cannot handle success because they cannot handle others talking about them. The higher you go up, the more people watch you. The higher your profile, the more people do not like you. However, it is also true that the more people see you, the more they like you. To be successful, you must focus on who likes you, not on who dislikes you. Every relationship or encounter will not lead to the kind of fruitfulness you expect—even when God places you in the situation.

When God elevates you, it can lead to depression if you do not handle it in the right way. For example, do you know that 75 percent of the people who win the lottery are either broke, dead or in a mental institution five years later? Having a lot of money is great, but great wealth also brings a lot of other problems. Success is wonderful, but the blessing carries a burden.

First Corinthians 10:11 tells us that we are to learn from the things that happened in the Bible. Everything that happened in the Bible occurred to teach us a lesson. What often hinders us is that we read the Bible for history instead of application. We read God's Word for

Every relationship or encounter will not lead to the kind of fruitfulness that you expect— even when God places you in the situation.

knowledge, but not for experience. When you read about Paul and Silas in a Philippian jail, you should discover your Philippian jail. When you read about Jesus on the cross, you should find your cross. What is your fiery furnace? What is your Red Sea? Everything that is recorded in the Bible is there so we can learn from it.

Overcoming Depression

There are people in the Bible who went through periods of depression, but thankfully, they overcame it. Here are some proven, biblically sound ways for God's people to overcome depression.

1. Consistent Revelation

If you are to overcome depression, you need to consistently hear from God. First Kings 19:5 says, "*And he lay and slept under a juniper tree and an angel touched him and said...*" Then, in verse 7, "*The angel of the Lord came the second time and touched him and said...*" Elijah was also in communication with the Lord in verse 9, "*The word of the Lord came to him, and he said unto him, 'What doest thou here, Elijah?'*" Then in verse 11, "*And he said 'Go forth, and stand upon the mount...*"

You cannot overcome depression by yourself. You are a prime candidate for depression when you stop reading God's Word or having morning devotion with God. You are a prime candidate for depression when you get hooked on songs more than the Word. You have to hear from God. God will talk to you even when you are depressed. Why is that important? Because most people do not want to be around you when you are down, but God will always be with you. Although Elijah had just finished telling the Lord to kill him, the Lord was still with him under that juniper tree.

2. Correct Elevation

When the angel appeared, he told Elijah to stand. He did not tell him to go to the latest church conference. He did not tell him to go to church. The angel's command to Elijah suggests that there are times when we think God is telling us to do something spiritual, but in reality He is telling us to do the practical.

When the angel met Elijah, he was lying down. Then he got up, ate and laid down again. He ate because God had provided. It is the same with us. Sometimes we get up long enough to receive God's provisions, but when it is time to do His will, we lie down. We get up to get the job, but we lie down when it comes to arriving there on time. We get up to get the blessing, but we lie down when it is time to bless someone else. We get up to receive, but we lie down when it is time to give. We focus more on God's giving than on doing His will.

The angel came back and told Elijah to get up. When he got up, God told him to go and stand before Him on the mountain. God was saying, "I don't want you on your knees, I want you on your feet." Some saints are guilty of staying on their knees as a substitute for getting on their feet. Some saints are guilty of acting when they should be praying and praying when they should be acting. Just because you are elevated, does not mean you are elevated correctly.

3. Continuous Mobilization

The root word of mobilization is *mobile*, which means "to keep moving." When it is time for you to stand, it is also time for you to walk. Elijah got up and moved. Therefore, I believe that depression is always greater when you are not doing anything. People generally become depressed at night more than during the day because things slow down at night. When things slow down, the mind has time to think about those things that can lead to depression.

I remember a difficult time in my ministry. I came home after a business meeting at church and drifted into a pity party. I asked myself, "Why are people so mean? All I've ever tried to do, Lord..." The Lord stopped me and said, "Not now. Don't go there. I want you to focus on how far I've brought you. I want you to focus on where I have you and where I want you to go. Don't get caught up in what has happened to you. Look at where you are and where you are going."

When depression comes your way, you cannot slow down. That is when you have to pick up the pace.

When depression comes your way, you cannot slow down. That is when you have to pick up the pace. As soon as you start your little pity party, that is when you start focusing on things that are beyond your control. You must tell yourself, "It didn't work out, but *all things work together for the good for those who love the Lord...*" (Romans 8:28), and *"greater is He that is in me than he that is in the world"* (I John 4:4). Sometimes you have to talk yourself into being happy. The important thing is to keep moving. If one church disappoints you, find another church. If one man lets you down, find another man. If one job lets you down, find another job. Be continuously mobile.

When you are depressed, be careful not to think you are the only one who has troubles.

4. Clear Observation

In verse 10, Elijah perceived that he was the only prophet left. When you are depressed, be careful not to think you are the only one who has troubles. Likewise, when things are going well, do not think you are the only one doing well. When you are living right, do not fall into thinking that you are the only one living right. Sometimes we think, "Nobody loves God, but me. Nobody wants to live holy, but me. Nobody wants to do the right thing, but me."

Whenever you make yourself the center of attention, you have entered into sin. The middle letter in sin is "I." When Elijah said, "I'm the only one left," (I Kings 19:10) God replied, "Elijah, I have seven thousand who are living holy, who love me and are doing my will" (I Kings 19:18). Whenever you think you are the only one, God will let you know that there are seven thousand more. One of the devil's tricks is to make you believe that you are the only one experiencing what you are going through. It is good for people to actively engage in small support groups because they can see that they are not alone. Have you ever talked to someone who started telling you his or her problems? You probably found that their problems made yours look small. Sometimes you need to hear that others do not have money, are down, that their marriage is on the rocks or that they lost a job.

Do not ever think you are the only person doing well or doing poorly. Do not think that God is blessing only you, nor should you ever think that God is only blessing the Joneses. Be happy whenever God blesses anyone. God's people do not have to compete for His favor. We do not have to out-sing, out-teach or out-preach anyone. All we have to do is be ourselves. It is not about competing. It is about giving God the glory and lifting up His name.

5. Committed Associations

Beginning with I Kings 19:15, the Lord gives Elijah the names of three people to anoint—Hazael, who will be king over

Syria; Jehu, who will be king over Israel; and Elisha, who will replace Elijah.

Elijah anointed the first king so he could do something externally. The second king was anointed to do something internally. Elisha was anointed for the eternal. Sometimes God aligns you with people who can help you with external things. Sometimes He will join you with people to help you with internal matters. At other times, He will join you with people to help you with matters that are eternal. When Elijah anointed Elisha, the younger prophet's job was to be committed to his mentor.

Interestingly, from this point on, you never see Elijah depressed again. Why did Elijah need a committed association? Because he ran from the servant he previously had. Sometimes you may find yourself running from the people that God sends you. After God joined Elijah and Elisha, they were always together. There should be someone in your life with whom you are bound by the Spirit of God. It does not have to be anyone in your church. Unfortunately, some of us come to church looking for friends instead of fellowship.

There are some people God puts in your life to be with you no matter what comes. Let me warn you here: Stay away from people who say to you, "I'm with you as long as you're right." That is a warning sign because nobody is always right. Anyone can be there when everything is going well, but what happens when you have lost everything? You need someone strong enough to tell you, "You're as wrong as two left shoes, but I'm going to stick with you anyway. I'm going to encourage you out of this thing. You're still my brother. You're still my sister. We're in this thing together, but wrong is wrong." The person who is with you will not gossip about you and publicize your business. Someone who is really with you will not tear you down. This is the kind of friend you need. This is the kind of marriage partner you need.

In II Kings 2:10, Elijah told Elisha, "If you see me when I'm taken from you, you'll get a double anointing of my power." Afterward, wherever you see Elijah, you see Elisha. As Elijah was taken up to heaven, he threw down his mantle and Elisha received a double portion of his anointing. Elijah did eight miracles, but Elisha did sixteen.

Beware of leaving the places and people where God has placed you. Do not have so much pride that when you are wrong you cannot turn around and go back. Do not let people run you away from where God has placed you. When you remove yourself from where God has placed you, you can lose your anointing, your power and whatever God is doing in your life.

You need someone in your life who will stick with you no matter what happens. Even if you find a person like that on earth, you still

When you remove yourself from where God has placed you, you can lose your anointing, your power, and whatever God is doing in your life.

have one in heaven—His name is Jesus. He is a friend who sticks closer than a brother.

Depression is real, but it can be overcome. It can even affect people who are children of God. To overcome depression, you must **seek** God, **submit** to His voice, **step** according to His will, **see** that you are not alone and **surround** yourself with committed people.

CHAPTER THREE

Winning The Battle Over
FEAR

— II Kings 19:14–29 —

An excellent model of how to win the battle over fear is found in II Kings 19. Before you can understand how to overcome fear, it is necessary to first put our biblical story in its historic and political perspective.

The main character of the story found in II Kings 19 is Hezekiah, the king of Israel. By the time of Hezekiah's rule, the great United Kingdom that was ruled by David and his son Solomon was demolished. The Israelites were divided into two separate kingdoms—Israel, the Northern Kingdom, and Judah, the Southern Kingdom. Israel had ten tribes while Judah was comprised of only two. Hezekiah ruled over Judah. Meanwhile, Israel was defeated by the Assyrians and so the only group left was Judah and King Hezekiah.

As you read II Kings 19, you will discover three things:

- Hezekiah's report
- Hezekiah's reaction
- Hezekiah's results

Hezekiah received a report that the powerful and mighty Sennacherib, king of Assyria, was coming to fight him.

Hezekiah's reaction to the report starts in II Kings 19:1: *"And it came to pass, when king Hezekiah heard it, that he rent his clothes, and covered himself with sackcloth, and went into the house of the LORD."* What did he hear that made him tear his royal clothing, cover himself with sackcloth and go to the Temple? He heard that the king of Assyria meant to destroy Judah and Hezekiah knew that he could do it.

Verse 2 continues to describe Hezekiah's reaction to the news: *"And he sent Eliakim, which was over the household, and Shebna the scribe, and the elders of the priests, covered with sackcloth, to Isaiah the prophet the son of Amoz."* First, Hezekiah went into the house of God, then he sent someone else to go get the word of God from the prophet and bring it back to him. The prophet's job was to ensure that the king did what God wanted. This suggests that when your back is up against the wall, you need the house of God and the Word of God.

The royal messengers told Isaiah the news, "Sennacherib is coming after Judah" (II Kings 19:3), but Isaiah did not panic. He did not tear his clothing or put on sackcloth. Instead, he said, "Tell Hezekiah that everything is going to be alright. Tell Hezekiah not to be afraid because God is going to do something. God is going to cause the king of Assyria to be distracted while he's on his way to destroy Hezekiah. While Sennacherib is getting ready to destroy Hezekiah and Judah, God is going to cause trouble at his house. God is going to cause Sennacherib so much trouble that he will have to turn around and forget all about Hezekiah (II Kings 19:6–7).

After Hezekiah's reaction, came the results. After having gotten a word of hope from the prophet of God, Hezekiah began seeing the results. What God said would happen is exactly what happened. As Sennacherib was on his way to whip Hezekiah, trouble arose in his homeland and he had to turn back to deal with it. God can be trusted to keep His Word.

By this time, Hezekiah was feeling pretty good. But a little while later, Hezekiah received a letter from one of Sennacherib's workers that said, "We're still going to defeat you. We've been delayed, but we won't be denied. We did not come when we wanted to, but we're going to be there on time" (II Kings 19:9–13). The letter brought back Hezekiah's fear. This suggests that in life, trouble just keeps on coming. Just because you got over something one time, does not mean it is gone for good.

What Causes Fear?

Hezekiah received the letter and then the fear came. Before I share the ways that fear can be overcome, I want to explain five ways that fear can enter your life. When you study and meditate on II Kings 19, you will find each of these five methods.

1. Words That Are Written

Why did Hezekiah get scared? He read a letter. Sometimes you can be frightened by things you read. Some examples are: unemployment letters, denial of credit applications, student loan paybacks and children's report cards. These written forms of communication can cause fear to come into your life.

2. Words That Are Spoken

Hezekiah was worried because he heard the Assyrians say, "We're going to get you. You're going to get a beat down." Sometimes spoken words can cause fear. People can say things that frighten you.

3. What You Have Witnessed

What Hezekiah saw scared him. He knew that whenever the Assyrians said they were going to whip someone, they did it. He had already witnessed Israel, his own people in the Northern Kingdom as well as other nations, taken out by the Assyrians. In real life, you can see things that cause fear. Even things on the news can cause you to become afraid.

4. Wickedness

Not only did Hezekiah see that the Assyrians did not play, he also knew that they were very wicked. They neither believed in God, nor trusted Him. They served false gods, and did whatever they wanted to please themselves. They were so wicked that when they captured another nation, they would tie up the men and make them watch as they raped their wives and daughters. Then, they would untie the men, put them up on a big building and slide them down a razor blade into a pool of alcohol. That was wicked! When they destroyed a nation, they would cut off their heads and take them over to the next nation. They would put the heads at the boundary line of that nation as a way of saying, "Do you want some of this?" They were so wicked that when God told Jonah to run revival in Nineveh, Jonah declined. Do you know why Jonah declined? He refused to go because Nineveh was in Assyria. Jonah basically was saying, "I don't mind running revival at a local church, but I'm not interested in going to Nineveh!"

Wicked people can scare you. Treacherous people who do not fear God or man can scare you.

5. Worry

It is possible for you to become so fearful that you are paralyzed and cannot perform even your normal activities. You can become so consumed in the affairs of others, so consumed in the things that could happen, so consumed in hypothetical scenarios, that you cannot do anything. If we were to be honest, we would have to admit there are some things going on in our lives that frighten us. In any close relationship, both parties should desire to know each other's fears. Why? Because

It is possible for you to become so fearful that you are paralyzed and cannot perform even your normal activities.

many of us have a tough time talking about our fears.

As men, we often fake bravery by pretending we do not have any fears. We say, "I'm not scared of anything." Look at what Hezekiah did in II Kings 19:14–16:

When you are scared, you have to do things that makes sense.

> *"And Hezekiah received the letter of the hand of the messengers, and read it: and Hezekiah went up into the house of the Lord, and spread it before the Lord. And Hezekiah prayed before the Lord, and said, O Lord God of Israel, which dwellest between the cherubims, thou art the God, even thou alone, of all the kingdoms of the earth; thou hast made heaven and earth. Lord, bow down thine ear, and hear: open, Lord, thine eyes, and see: and hear the words of Sennacherib, which hath sent him to reproach the living God."*

In essence, Hezekiah said, "God, it's not my problem. It's your problem. They're not coming against me. They're coming against you. They're not trying to take me out. They're trying to take you out." Whenever you make your problems God's problems, God will defend Himself. God will not let anyone beat Him. God will not let anyone defeat Him or make Him look like a fool.

Hezekiah was smart enough to say, "God, I'm turning it over to you." He said, "Open your ear and hear, open your eyes and look at what they said about You, God." To make matters worse, part of the letter said, "Hezekiah, if you think your God is going to help you, that's what the other nations said, too" (II Kings 19:12). They did not know that Hezekiah's God was a different God. They did not know that Hezekiah's God created the heavens and earth. Hezekiah had a God who would not lose or back down. Hezekiah did not have a God that he made, but a God who made him. You need a God like that!

How to Overcome Fear

1. Do Something Logical

Hezekiah did the same thing that you have to do to overcome fear—he did something logical. In other words, when you are scared, you have to do things that make sense. The root word of logical is *logic*. When you act logically, you do something understandable, something that makes sense, something that is comprehensible. The first thing Hezekiah did in II Kings 19:14 was go to church. Although he was threatened and scared, he went to church.

When your back is up against the wall, that is the time to be in church. When your money is funny and your change is strange, that is the time to be in church. When you do not know how you will pay your bills or your marriage is on the rocks, that is the time to be in church. It makes sense to go to church when you are not doing well, are in a bad mood, or when things are just not right. It does not make sense to stay at home playing with the remote or to hang out at the mall. It does not make sense to miss church on the Lord's Day because you are not feeling well. Somewhere between the beginning of church and the end of church, it is possible to be revived, to get some pep in your step and some pride in your stride. Do not let anyone or anything make you miss church.

Hezekiah went to the house of the Lord. He did not go to McDonald's, because when you are in trouble, a shake will not bring you out. He did not buy a lottery ticket, because there are some things the lottery cannot solve. When you are in trouble, you need to go where you can hear that everything is going to be alright. You need to go where can you hear, *"Weeping may endure for a night, but joy comes in the morning" (Psalm 30:5).* You

When your back is up against the wall, that is the time to be in church.

need to go someplace where you can hear, *"Greater is He that is in you, than he that is in the world" (I John 4:4).* You need to go where you can hear, *"No weapon formed against you shall prosper" (Isaiah 54:17).* Do something logical: stay in church.

2. Do Something Practical

Second Kings 19:15 says that Hezekiah prayed. He took practical action. Doing something practical means doing something useful and tangible. It means doing something that can be seen. Practical is from the root word *practice.* So practical means something you can put into practice, something that you can apply. The text says, *"He prayed"(II Kings 19:15).* Hezekiah was scared and in trouble, and he prayed. He did not know how or when God was going to work it out, but he prayed.

This is the way God operates: God says, "If you do what you can, I'll do what you can't. But why should I do what you can't, when you won't do what you can?" God tells us that He moves like this: "If you fill out the application, I'll touch the employer's heart. If you apply for that car or house, I'll cause the computer to show your credit as A+, and then I'll straighten it out after you sign the papers." You cannot limit God. You cannot put God in a box. All you can do is what you can do. You cannot make people like you, but you can like them. You cannot make people speak to you, but you can speak to them. Look at your day, today. Let us start with this morning. You brushed your teeth. God did not do that for you. You bathed yourself. God did not do that for you. You got dressed and got into your car, not God. Why did you do all of those things? Because there are some things you can do for yourself. Who woke you up this morning? God. Why? Because you cannot do that for yourself. He regulated your mind so you could dress properly. God made sure that an oncoming car did not cross over from the other lane and cause a head-on collision because you could not do that. If you do what you can, He will always do what you cannot. What sometimes hinders us is that we do not do anything practical. We fail to do what we can, and then wonder why we are not blessed.

3. Do Something Radical

Doing something radical means doing something that goes against the norm, something that goes against tradition. Radical means something that takes you out of your comfort zone, something that is off the chain. Hezekiah did something radical in II Kings 19:14. He opened the letter, read it and then the text says, he *"spread it before the Lord."* He read the letter and got scared, so he took it to the Temple and said, "God, read this. God, take a look at this. God, this is some foolishness. Don't You agree?"

I am suggesting that sometimes you ought to pull out your bills, and after reading them, say, "God, see this Macy's bill. God, see how much I owe American Express. God, see the Texaco statement." There may be times when you need to spread your children before God. At other times, you may need to spread your spouse, supervisor or other co-workers before the Lord. Better yet, there may come a time when you will need to spread yourself before the Lord and say, "It's me, O Lord, standing in the need of a breakthrough."

You have to be willing to do something radical. You can miss your blessing while trying to be cute, cool, slick and sophisticated. You can miss your blessing while trying to keep your makeup from running. As good as God has been to you, sometimes you ought to not worry about your makeup and just wipe it off. That is radical!

Everybody in the Bible who did something radical, received something radical. Look at Zacchaeus in Luke 19. He wanted to see Jesus so badly that he did something radical—he climbed a sycamore tree. Jesus passed by and Zacchaeus was looking down as Jesus was looking up. (When you look for Him, He will look for you.) Jesus went to Zacchaeus' house and blessed him. Jesus saved Zacchaeus' soul because he did something radical.

Mark 5 tells the story of the woman with the issue of blood. She said, "I'm tired of going to doctors. They haven't done a thing to help me. They just keep giving me new prescriptions, but this medicine isn't helping me one little bit. I'm sick and tired of being sick and tired. I'm going to do something radical, today!" She got up and touched the hem of Jesus' garment. When she touched His garment, power came out of Jesus and healed her infirmity. That is radical!

If you go back to Mark 2, you will read about four men who decided to do something radical. A paralytic's four friends wanted him to be healed. They said, "We need to get him to Jesus, so we'll have to do something radical." They went to the place where Jesus was teaching and preaching. Imagine if that happened today—four men bringing their paralyzed friend in the church so he can be healed, but an old mean usher meets them at the door saying, "You should have gotten here earlier. You have no business being late. We don't have any room. We can put you in the overflow room." But they say, "No way, Usher. We're going to do something radical. We're going up on the roof." The Bible says they tore the roof off of the house. These men knew what it meant to do something radical. Sometimes you have do something radical like run around the church praising God. As long as you do the norm, you will get the norm.

As you discern your radical action, remember that what is radical for you, may not be radical for someone else. Your radical is based on who you are. For some of you, radical means coming to church every Sunday because you are not doing that now. For others, radical means getting to church early because you come late. For still others, radical means not sleeping in church. You feel good while the choir is singing, but as soon as the preacher gets up, you remember you only had three hours of sleep last night. Radical for some of you means speaking to someone before that person speaks to you. Radical for some of you means accepting Christ as your Savior and joining the church when the invitation is extended. Being radical means making changes so things can change for you.

After Hezekiah spread that letter before God and prayed, II Kings 19:20 says:

> *"Then Isaiah the son of Amoz sent to Hezekiah, saying, Thus saith the Lord God of Israel, That which thou hast prayed to me against Sennacherib king of Assyria I have heard."*

Verse 32 continues:

> *"Therefore thus saith the Lord concerning the king of Assyria, He shall not come into this city, nor shoot an arrow there, nor come before it with shield, nor cast a bank against it."*

God said Sennacherib was not even going to come into the city, shoot an arrow or come before it with a shield, nor cast a bank against it. Verse 33 explains that the ruler of Assyria would leave the same way he came. God would defend the city (II Kings 19:34). In other words, God said "Sennacherib is coming against Me and I'm going to whip him. He thinks he's picking on you, but he's really coming against Me. So I will defeat him for My sake—to show him I don't play that."

Verse 35 reveals how God kept His Word. God did not make threats, instead He acted.

> *"And it came to pass that night, that the angel of the Lord went out, and smote in the camp of the Assyrians an hundred fourscore and*

five thousand: and when they arose early in the morning, behold, they were all dead corpses" (II Kings 19:35).

So Sennacherib, the king of Assyria, left Judah and headed home. Sennacherib had 185,000 soldiers in his army, but they were all dead by the next morning. Having no army, Sennacherib decided to retreat to his home city of Nineveh. As if losing his whole army was not bad enough, verse 37 shows that God was not through with him yet. Sennacherib's sons killed him with his own sword.

When you involve God in your problems, when you make it a God thing and not a "my" thing, God will always show up and fight your battles. Hezekiah never had to deal with Sennacherib again.

What's holding you back right now? Could it be that you are not doing enough logical, practical and radical things? It is not logical to keep using drugs. It just doesn't make sense! It is not practical to want a job, but never go out and seriously look for one. It is not radical to want a positive change in your life, but not involve God. Remember II Timothy 1:7 says, *"For God hath not given us the spirit of fear; but of power, and of love, and of a sound mind."*

Take control of your fears by vowing to continuously do something logical, practical and radical for the Lord.

CHAPTER FOUR

Winning The Battle Over
GRIEF

— The Book of Ruth —

The Book of Ruth deals with a lot of practical issues facing people today. Ruth addresses something that can be very problematic for many people. In Chapter 1, she is concerned with her mother-in-law. In Chapter 2, she faces unemployment. In Chapter 3, she copes with being single. In Chapter 4, she deals with married life. In a very real way, any of those four areas alone can cause great grief in a person's life. In-laws can bring grief. Certainly, unemployment can create great grief. Being single can lead to grief, but so can being married. Regardless of which chapters of Ruth's life you may experience, you will certainly encounter grief.

In this book, Ruth's losses are exposed and her labor detailed. The word labor often brings to mind the word *work*. In order to overcome grief or get over something you have lost, you will have to work at it. Grief is not just dealing with the feelings we experience when someone dies. In Chapter 1, we find Ruth has lost her husband, father-in-law and brother-in-law to death and her sister to distance. Overcoming grief can include people, places and possessions.

After experiencing these tragedies while living in the city of Moab, Ruth's mother-in-law, Naomi, decided to move back to Bethlehem. She told her two daughters-in-law, Ruth and Orpah, "You stay here because there are no men in Bethlehem for you to marry. I'm so old now that even if I had another son, by the time the child became grown, you would be too old to marry him" (Ruth 1:8–9). Orpah decided not to go with Naomi, thinking she would have a better chance of finding another husband, but Ruth told her, "Please don't ask me to leave you. Wherever you go, I'll go. Wherever you stay, I'll stay. Your people will be my people. Your God will be my God" (Ruth 1:16). Ruth went to Bethlehem with her mother-in-law.

When Ruth moved from Moab to Bethlehem, she left her comfort zone. All of her friends were in Moab. She lost her familiar surroundings, her sister and her spouse, but she did not lose her sense. If you hang on to your sense in the midst of your situation, everything will be alright.

Chapter 1 describes some things that Ruth did to handle her loss. In the opening chapter, we see Ruth weeping. Verse 14 says that she *"wept again,"* which suggests that it was not her first time crying. Tears are one way people handle grief. However, one cry will not get you over what you lost. Grieving is a process and one cry is not enough to heal a great loss—the death of a parent, the loss of a job, the loss of a relationship, the loss of a child, the loss of innocence, the loss of hope. In Chapter 1, you see Ruth weeping, but you also see her exercise wisdom after she finishes crying.

You cannot cry forever. At some point, you will have to exercise wisdom. Despite her tears, Ruth made a sound and wise choice to accompany her mother-in-law to Bethlehem. One thing that may have led Ruth to follow Naomi was the way Naomi handled her grief. Ruth recognized that Naomi had lost her husband and two sons, but she had not lost her sense. Ruth saw that God was on Naomi's side.

People watch how you handle losses. Some Christians think they can just testify by handing out cards that say "Jesus is the way." Some people think that they can testify by inviting everybody to their church. One powerful way to testify is to lose your job and not lose your mind. One way to testify is to have your child mess up, but you not be messed up because of it. Another way to testify is to have your husband show out, but you not do it too. Some people have a good testimony as long as everything is going well, but when things go wrong it is a different story. When things go wrong in your life, do you still have a smile on your face? Do you still have joy

Grieving is a process and one cry is not enough to heal a great loss.

in your heart? Do you still have peace in your soul?

Ruth used wisdom to make a choice. She told Naomi, "I'm sticking with you." Sometimes God will put people in your life who will stick with you, come hell or high water, and you will stick with them.

We see Ruth's weeping, then we see her wisdom and finally we see her will. In Ruth 1:19, she does what she said she was going to do. Some people talk a good game. They are always saying what they are going to do, but they never get around to actually doing it. Her weeping was her crying, her wisdom was her choice and her will was her commitment.

There comes a time in life when you have to stand and say, "I will."

There comes a time in life when you have to stand and say, "I will." David said *"I will bless the Lord at all times" (Psalm 34:1)*. The prodigal son said, *"I will arise and go to my father" (Luke 15:18)*. You just have to say "I will," and take another step down the path of righteousness.

Overcoming Grief

In Chapter 2, Ruth honors her commitment. Here are some steps you will have to take to bring yourself out of grief.

1. Plan Instead of Pouting

By Chapter 2, Ruth is living in Bethlehem. She and Naomi do not have a man to provide for them. In those days, the husband kept bread on the table and made sure there was money in the checking account. Since both of their husbands were gone, Ruth asked Naomi, "How do you feel about my getting a job?" (Ruth 2:2). She began planning so that life could get better for both of them. In essence Ruth was saying, "Naomi, I want to take care of you. I want to make life better for you. You don't have to be sad and upset forever. Although I'm not from here, I'm going into the field and work."

Ruth planned instead of pouting. We do not see her continuing to wallow in tears or pity. She should have had a husband to take care of her, but he was gone. She knew she had to get up and do something. When you are fired from your job, you have to do something. When your car stops running, you have to do something. Ruth decided to get a job instead of pouting.

Some people who come to me for counseling have one sad story after another. I always respond to them, "I know it's not fair. Yes, I know she shouldn't have done you that way. What is your plan?" "Yes, I know he did you wrong, but what's your plan?" You cannot remain a victim having a pity party.

Sometimes God will allow you to fall into a pit. The problem with some people is when they fall into a pit, they travel with this consonant called "Y." Not "why," but the letter "Y." While in our pit, we attach the letter "Y" to it and make our pit a pity party.

In the Indy 500, the first one around the track 500 times is declared the winner. No one can keep going around the track without stopping, so every now and then, they make a pit stop. The pit stop is not the place to complain, the pit stop is the place to gas up, get new tires and get new instructions. Sometimes God allows you to fall into a pit so He can do for you what the mountain highs and the good times cannot do. In the pit, you learn that *"Greater is He that is in me than he that is in the world"* (I John 4:4).

You have to handle your pit stops. Sometimes a hospital room is your pit stop. Sometimes the school calling you about your child is a pit stop. Sometimes a divorce or separation is a pit stop. Ruth said, "I'm not having a pity party. I'm going to find work."

2. Follow the Fruitful

Ruth got a job. She said *"Let me go to the field and glean"* (Ruth 2:2). There were reapers and gleaners in the field. The gleaners picked up what the reapers dropped. The only way a gleaner could be productive was by following a reaper. Ruth gleaned in the field after the reapers. A part of overcoming grief is following people who are productive because who you follow determines what you pick up. When you follow people who are doing negative things, you will pick up negative things, but when you follow people who are determined to go on, you pick up their attitude. I am careful about who I hang out with because I know that I cannot fly like an eagle, if I am running with turkeys. I have to be around people who want something out of life.

While teaching at Luther Rice Seminary in Atlanta, Georgia, one of my students asked me how I felt about pastors taking their members to other churches to see how they do things. I told the student that I highly recommend it as long as they visit a church that has more to offer. When you go places that do things better than you, it can motivate and inspire you, but when you hang around people who are trifling and lazy, they will soon pull you down. If you are trying to get out of debt, be around someone who wants to live debt-free. If you want to be an entrepreneur, then hang around someone who owns a business. If you want a good marriage, go around someone who already has a faithful marriage. You have to follow the fruitful. Follow people who are doing positive things.

Ruth went to work. She did not go to work and talk about "All My Children." When Ruth saw people who were not doing anything, she said, "That's not who I want to follow." Watch and decide carefully who you want to hang around. Everybody who goes to church is not fruitful. Sometimes the best wisdom you can exercise is finding out who to stay away from in your church. If you sit in a section where people are passing notes and talking about what someone else is wearing, you may need to change your seat.

3. Work Without Worrying

You cannot work and worry. You have to work and leave the details to God. Quit worrying about whether they are going to give you the contract. Quit worrying about whether they are going to hire you or fire you. Don't worry about whether they are going to like you. Quit worrying—just work.

When Ruth went into that field, she was only concerned with working. She worked so hard that the owner of the field, Boaz, asked "Who is that woman?" (Ruth 2:5).

Boaz was attracted to Ruth right away because she was working. She was not profiling. She was not playing with her hair or painting her nails. He never saw a tattoo or an earring in her tongue. He saw her working. Ruth's mindset was, "My husband died, and I'm not going to sit around talking about what I lost and what I don't have. I'm going to get out there and do what I can do. Then I'm going to let God do what I can't do. I'm going to get out here and work because I have to take care of Naomi."

Boaz's foreman told him, "She came to me this morning and asked if she could follow the reapers" (Ruth 2:7). From morning until then she did what she said she was going to do. Boaz said, "Don't let her leave." As the story of Ruth closes, Boaz marries Ruth and she and Naomi never have to work again. While she was concerned with taking care of someone else, the Lord sent someone to take care of her. God provided for her out of her faithfulness.

Ruth's experience suggests that you do not have to look for a mate, beg an employer to hire you or plead with someone to feed you. All you have to do is what God tells you to do. God will see to it that the right people come into your life. When God is on your side, you do not have to beg. You can ask all you want, but you do not have to beg. God's Word says, in Matthew 7:7, *"Ask and it shall be given you, seek and ye shall find, knock and it shall be opened."*

After Ruth married Boaz, you never hear her talking about her first husband. When you get what God wants you to have, there is no need to reflect on the past. Some people spend too much time talking about the past—what happened at the old church, the old pastor or the old neighborhood. Deal with where you are right now.

Ruth made five concrete moves to overcome the grief of her circumstances in Moab. First, she **moved on** by going from Moab to Bethlehem. There comes a time in life when you have to simply move on. If you are not growing in your local church, do not stay there complaining. It may just be time to move on. If you are in a relationship where it is evident that the other person does not

When God is on your side, you do not have to beg. You can ask all you want, but you do not have to beg.

appreciate you and just tolerates you, that is a good sign to move on. There comes a time to move on—from places, people and possessions.

The second thing Ruth did was she **moved with**. Ruth did no try to handle her situation alone. Just as God allowed Naomi to be there for Ruth, He has people to help you overcome your obstacles. You must decide to join with someone. Moses had Joshua. Elijah had Elisha. Paul had Silas. Jesus had His disciples. Who do you have? You need to move with because you cannot handle everything by yourself.

After moving on and moving with, the third thing Ruth did was to **move out**. In Chapter 2, Ruth said, "I have to get out of this house," and decided to go find work. It is always harder to overcome grief when you are sitting at home in your pajamas with the blinds closed. At some point, you have to open the blinds, get your teeth out of that glass and move on. At some point, you have to quit telling that sad story and step out of your comfort zone.

The fourth thing Ruth did was she began to **move around** people who were working. Misery loves company, but so does success. You need to be around people who, when you start telling them your sad story—again—will say, "Not today. We're not talking about that today." There are some people who are so stuck in something that no matter what the conversation is about, they can reach back and talk about the past.

The final thing Ruth did was to **move up**. Ruth moved up when she married Boaz. A lot of people in church talk about wanting to move to another level, but it costs to go to a higher level.

You do not just go to another level because you want to go there. Moving up may cost you some friends, fellowship, money and sacrifices. When you move to another level, you must be willing to let the chips fall where they may. You do not just move up. You have to learn to move on, move with, move out and move around before you can move up.

If you are grieving, you have to keep moving because it is hard to hit a moving target. When the devil comes after you, you want him to say, "Hey, where did you go?" Have you ever gone walking or running with someone who is determined to keep moving? You want to stop and get a coke or a sandwich, but they keep walking and exercising. You keep going because they keep going. If you are determined to keep moving, everybody will have to keep moving with you.

No matter where God takes you, there will be some people who cannot come along. You will have to tell them, "I love you and I'm not mad at you, but you are not headed where God is taking me. You were a blessing to me and you helped me, but I want what God wants me to have more than being with you."

When you move to another level, you must be willing to let the chips fall where they may.

When you want what God wants you to have, you can rely on Him when your back is up against the wall.

Grieving is a process. It can slow you down or even stop you dead in your tracks for awhile. It hurts to lose someone or something that you care about, but like Ruth, at some point you must decide that it is time to move on, move with, move out and move around so you can move up to the next level of blessings that God has for you.

CHAPTER FIVE

Winning The Battle Over
GUILT

— Luke 15:11–32 —

n important issue facing many of God's children is
how to overcome guilt. One of the things you will
discover in your Christian walk is that the devil has
a field day tormenting many believers with feelings of guilt.

The fifteenth chapter of the Gospel of Luke deals with
things that are lost. There is a story about a lost sheep in
verses 1–7. In verses 8–10, you will find the story of a lost
coin. Finally, verses 11–32 tell the story of a lost son, the
prodigal. All three were lost, but for different reasons. The
sheep was lost out of curiosity. It was just wandering and got
lost. The coin was lost out of carelessness and the prodigal
son was lost by choice.

The story of the lost son is the most detailed. Perhaps
Jesus made this story longer because most of the time
when we mess up, it is not out of curiosity or carelessness,
but choice. Without even knowing you, I guarantee you
that some of the things that have plagued your life have
been by choice.

Luke 15 teaches us in a very real way that there is some sheep, coin and prodigal son in all of us. Can you think of a time in your life when you messed up just by being curious? Curiosity has gotten many people hooked on drugs. Like the coin, many people have gotten lost carelessly. Untold numbers of women have gotten pregnant out of wedlock because of carelessness. However, the majority of us must admit we are lost by choice. By looking at the life lesson of the lost son, we can discover some valuable truths about winning the battle over guilt.

Beginning with Luke 15:11, you will learn five things about the son. First, you see his **home life**: *"And he said, a certain man had two sons."* From this short verse, we learn something important about the son's home life—he has a brother and a father.

The second thing we learn about is his **handout**. Verse 12 says, *"And the younger of them said to his father, Father, give me the portion of goods that falleth to me. And he divided unto them his living."* That means his father gave the money to him. It was a handout. Why was it a handout? The son did not deserve it, earn it or work for it. It was a free will gift from his father.

Can you think of a time in your life when you messed up just by being curious?

When you read Luke 15:13–14, the third thing you see is the son's **haughtiness**. What does it mean to be haughty? It means to be prideful, selfish and arrogant. Look at the son's haughtiness in these verses:

> *"And not many days after the younger son gathered all together, and took his journey into a far country, and there wasted his substance with riotous living. And when he had spent all, there arose a mighty famine in that land; and he began to be in want"* (Luke 15:13–14).

Do you see his haughtiness? Who is he living for in verses 13–14? Nobody, but himself. He is very haughty.

The fourth thing you discover about this son is his **hog pen**. In Luke 15:15–19, you find him in the hog pen feeding pigs while he is hungry himself. Verses 15–16 read:

> *"And he went and joined himself to a citizen of that country; and he sent him into his fields to feed swine. And he would fain have filled his belly with the husks that the swine did eat: and no man gave unto him."*

According to verses 17–19, while in the hog pen, he evaluates his situation and makes plans to return home.

Finally, you see the prodigal son's **happiness**. As sad as this story gets, all is not lost. There is good news. In verse 20, you see the son's happiness restored. To make a long story short, he returns home and is unconditionally accepted by his dad.

The lesson for us is to be careful how you handle your home life and handouts because handling them incorrectly can lead you to haughtiness or a hog pen, and adversely affect your happiness.

There is nothing wrong with having desires; however, you have to be careful with your desires.

What Causes Guilt?

The story of the prodigal son is one with which most Christians can identify. At some point in life, all of us have thought we were missing out on something because we were living under our father's rules. Like the prodigal, if we do not find another way to seek fulfillment, the only things we will end up with are feelings of guilt and sorrow.

Luke 15 reveals five things that can cause feelings of guilt. Just as there are five things that can cause guilt, there are five ways to overcome these feelings.

1. Desires

What did the lost son desire? In Luke 15:12, he told his father, "Give me what belongs to me." In the Bible days, the father was responsible for saving an inheritance to give his children at the appropriate time. What hurt this young man was that he wanted his share before it was time. He wanted it before he was able to handle it. There is nothing wrong with having desires; however, you have to be careful with your desires. The Bible says *"He shall give thee the desires of thine heart," (Psalm 37:4).* However, your desire becomes a problem when you want it before it is time. Untimely desires can lead to guilt.

2. Decisions

In Luke 15:13, after the son received what he desired, he made a decision: *"And not many days after the younger son gathered all together."* As soon as he got what he wanted, he put all of his things in a bag because he decided to leave. After we review the third action that leads to guilt, you will discover how causes one, two and three always go together.

3. Departures

An untimely departure can cause feelings of guilt. Verse 13 continues, *"...and took his journey into a far country."* The son decided that home was not good enough. He thought, "I need to leave here because the grass is greener on the other side." He figured he could do better somewhere else than what he was doing at home. So, he left.

What was home? His home was his place of protection and refuge. His home was his place of covering, provision, and most importantly, the place to which God had assigned him. This suggests that when you prematurely depart from where God has assigned you, guilt is coming down the road.

What led to his departure? His decision. What led to his decision? His desires. You need to seriously pray about your desires.

4. Delights

Luke 15:13 reveals that he not only received his fortune and departed into a far country, but once there he wasted his substance on riotous living. He started living a life of leisure. He became a big baller, a shot caller. He lived for what felt good, enjoyable and pleasurable to him. All of it led to guilt.

5. Disasters

Luke 15:14 says, *"When he had spent all, there arose a mighty famine in that land and he began to be in want."* Verse 13 says he wasted and verse 14 says he wanted. What you waste today, you will want tomorrow. Have you ever wasted money and later wanted it back? Have you wasted time and later wanted it back? Have you wasted a relationship or an opportunity and later wanted it back? The prodigal son lost his fortune and began to want. From that point on, he felt guilty. In verse 17, he had a revelation: *"When he came to himself, he said, 'How many hired servants of my father's have bread enough and to spare, and I perish with hunger!'"*

Do you see guilt there? What was he really saying? He was reflecting on all that he had lost. He started realizing that he had been careless with more than just the money. He realized the value of what he left at his father's house. He was saying, "I left it all! At home, I had cable, a Sony PlayStation and a bed. At home, I had someone praying for me. I had a covering."

To whom was he speaking? Himself. Where was he as he talked to himself? In the hog pen, which suggests that God will allow you to meet the hog pen so you can meet yourself. This young man started thinking in the hog pen. He said, "I messed up. I blew it." What did he say in verses 18–19?

> "I will arise and go to my father, and will say unto him, Father, I have sinned against heaven, and before thee. And am no more worthy to be called thy son: make me as one of thy hired servants."

In verse 12, he told his father, "Give me," but in verses 18–19, he just wanted to be a servant in his father's house. He got up and went to his father. He did not know what to expect when he got home, but he was willing to endure whatever he had to in order to live under the shelter of his father's house. Maybe he expected to be ridiculed or rejected. Maybe he expected to be chastised.

Luke 15:20–21 gives us a glimpse into the tearful reunion between father and son:

> "But when he was yet a great way off, his father saw him, and had compassion, and ran, and fell on his neck, and kissed him. And the son said unto him, Father, I have sinned against heaven, and in thy sight, and am no more worthy to be called thy son."

After this, you do not see the son or the father dealing with guilt again. The son does not condemn himself again, nor does his father condemn him. You never see the son beating himself over the head again.

How many times have you had to deal with feelings of guilt? Truthfully, all of us have to deal with feelings of guilt from time to time. Now, I will share how to overcome guilt.

Overcoming Feelings of Guilt

One emotion that the enemy uses to distract, deceive, dismantle and defeat believers is guilt. What is guilt? Guilt is overly condemning yourself for your wrongdoing. You ought to feel bad when you do wrong, but when you overly condemn yourself, Satan is using guilt against you.

Someone from our new member's class once asked me, "How often should I get baptized?" I told them that one time was enough. Then the person asked, "Well, can I get baptized again?" And I said, "Yes, you can be baptized again, but it depends on the circumstances." So I gave the class a personal illustration: I accepted Christ when I was ten years old. I knew what I was doing. I came home, I told my brother, Kevin. He said, "You can't get baptized before I do!" So the next Sunday he went down and did what I did. I accepted Christ for the right reason. Kevin did it because he felt that as the older brother, he should be baptized before me. Four or five years later, Kevin met a guy on the street who witnessed to him. After hearing him, Kevin accepted Christ. The guy told him that he needed to be baptized. My brother told him that he had already been baptized, but after further discussion, Kevin realized that he was baptized for the wrong reason. So he decided to be baptized again.

I have also known people who walked away from God, stayed a long time and then came back to Him. As a sign of their commitment, they rededicated themselves to Christ and were baptized again. Someone else in the class asked, "Should we get baptized every time we do something wrong?" I told them, if that was the case, we might as well leave the pool on all the time. Guilt tells you that you have to be baptized every time you do something wrong. Everyone experiences feelings of guilt at one time or another in life, but there are steps you can take so guilt will not consume and overcome you.

There are steps you can take so guilt will not consume and overcome you.

1. Acknowledge Your Wrong

In Luke 15:17, the prodigal son acknowledged that he had done wrong. He came to himself and realized that even his father's servants had more than enough bread to spare while he was starving to death. Some of you have come to everybody, but yourself. You have come to the job, the man, the woman, the kids, but you need to come to yourself. Overcoming guilt begins with acknowledging to yourself that you have done wrong.

2. Admit Your Wrong to Others

After the prodigal son acknowledged his wrongdoing to himself, he needed to make amends with the people he had hurt. In Luke 15:18 he said, *"I will arise and go to my father and tell him that I've done wrong."* First, he said to himself, "You've hurt yourself." Secondly, he said, "I'm going to tell my father 'I'm sorry.'" How many people do you know who can acknowledge their wrongdoing to themselves, but cannot confess it to the person they hurt? There is another group of people who can say, "I'm sorry," but are never totally honest with themselves about their wrongdoing.

He said, "I'm going to go to my dad and say, 'I'm sorry that I hurt you.'" The prodigal's actions suggest that when you get yourself straight, you should feel compelled to get it straight with others. If you cannot get it straight with other people, it is a sign that things are not right within you. Most people cannot get it right with themselves because they like to blame others for their mistakes.

Over-coming guilt begins with acknowl-edging to yourself that you have done wrong.

It is like this: If I drive a Honda Accord and it stops on a busy section of an interstate, that is not the time for me to bad mouth all Hondas. It does not make sense because while I am badmouthing all Hondas, other Hondas are passing me by. At that point, I need to get under my hood and see what is causing the problem. In other words, if a man has messed over a woman, that is not the time to dog all men, but it might be the time for the woman to check herself and see why those things keep happening to her. She can keep saying, "It didn't work with husband one and it didn't work with husband two and it didn't work with husband three," but there is one common denominator in all of those failed relationships—her!

3. Accept the Consequences of Your Wrong

After the son admitted his wrongdoing to himself and apologized to his father, he went a step further. He was willing to accept the consequences of leaving home and coming back flat broke. In Luke 15:19 he said, "I'm going to ask my dad to make me a hired servant. I left home a son, but I'm willing to come back and work as a servant." He left home in good standing, but he was willing to go back as a slave.

Why is that important? Because many times we are led to believe "If I apologize, it's all over." This phenomena is most amazing to me when I am involved in marital counseling with church members. For example, the husband will have done something to cause the couple to seek counseling. When he apologizes for what he did, he expects everything to return to business as usual. Then, he has the unmitigated gall to get an attitude and try to flip the script on his wife to make her feel like she is the one with the problem. God will forgive all sin, but there are always consequences for our sin. Do you remember the fall of Samson in Judges 16? God forgave Samson and gave him another chance, but he was still blind because of his foolish choices. Overcoming guilt means you have to be willing to accept the consequences of what you have done wrong.

4. Act On Straightening Out Your Wrong

Notice that the son started talking to himself in Luke 15:17 while he was still in the hog pen. He was sitting down in verse 17, but the first three words of verse 18 are, *"I will arise."* The first three words of verse 20 are: *"And he arose."* Some people get from verse 17 to verse 18, and never go forward to verse 20. They are always saying, "I will," but never get to "I did."

The son is talking to himself in verses 17–19. Why do you think he spent so much time talking to himself? What was he really doing? He was practicing and encouraging himself. He was motivating himself so he could do what he knew he needed to do.

I am suggesting that sometimes you have to talk to yourself to strengthen *yourself.* If you have ever fasted, you know that you may have to tell yourself, "Don't open it," when you walk past the refrigerator. You may not even like fast food, but when you are fasting the aroma makes that hamburger smell irresistible. To successfully fast, you have to keep telling yourself, "I'm going to do this thing." If you have ever decided to lose weight or start an exercise regimen, you had to talk to yourself first. You must strengthen yourself by talking to yourself.

The son strengthened himself by talking to himself, and then in verse 20 he acted on his talk by getting up and going to his father. He did not know what to expect, but the repentant son was willing to accept the consequences of his choices. He was not sure how his father would respond to his return. However, verse 20 tells us that the father met his son halfway as he approached the house.

This parable is a picture of God's forgiveness. It suggests that when you decide to get your act straight, God will meet you halfway. The father did not go out looking for his son, nor did he hire someone to find him and say "Come home." The father waited until his son made up his mind to return home. Why? Because the son decided to leave on his own, the father knew that his son had to make his own decision to come back.

Sometimes we get people to do right when it is not their decision. The father met his son halfway, and then kissed and embraced him. What do you think went through the son's mind when his dad greeted him that way? "Everything is alright." What could he have done? He could have said, "Dad, I'm so glad you're glad to see me. Where's my bed?," but instead in verse 21, he confessed to his father, *I have sinned.* Would you have confessed your sin to your father after such a warm reception?

5. Ask for Forgiveness for Your Wrong

You have to confess to people, "I did you wrong. I apologize. Will you forgive me?" You hurt yourself when you try to receive forgiveness by apologizing in a sly way. Instead of confessing their wrong and openly seeking forgiveness, some people will say, "If I've done anything..." If? How many times do people say, "I probably said some things that I shouldn't have..." Probably? "I might have done something that offended you..." Might? How about saying, "What I did was wrong. I apologize. Will you forgive me?"

After asking for forgiveness, you need to go a step further. After the person forgives you, then say, "And I pledge that I'll try hard not to let it happen again." Each step takes more humility than the last. It takes humility to take the first step—to seek them out. Then it takes humility to say, "I apologize." It takes another step of humility to ask, "Will you forgive me?" And another one to say, "I'm going to try my best to keep that from happening again."

The son asked his dad for forgiveness and the father forgave him. His father represents God. What does God say? *"Ye have not, because ye ask not" (James 4:2).* First John 1:9 says *"If you confess your sins, God is faithful and just to forgive you and to cleanse you from all unrighteousness."* There is no problem with God forgiving or cleansing, but before He does, you must confess. The Greek word for confess is *homologeo,* which means "to say it like God says it." For example, if you commit adultery, do not pray and tell the Lord, "I had an extramarital affair." Call it what God calls it—adultery. If your thing is homosexuality, if your bag is lesbianism, then you do not need to go to God and say, "I'm living an alternative lifestyle." We tend to dress up sin so that it sounds more palatable. God wants you to call it what it is—sin!

An extramarital affair—that almost sounds like a sport, doesn't it? It almost sounds as harmless as golf or basketball, like extracurricular activities. Many times, you may be plagued with guilt because you have not come clean with God. I believe that anyone who does not come clean with God will not come clean with other people.

We tend to dress up sin so that it sounds more palatable.

The Father's Response

Let us look at what the father did to welcome his son back into the fold.

The Father Received Him Blamelessly

What does that mean? He forgave him because he was his son. You are a child of God. Notice that the father did not hold anything over his son's head. He did not withhold forgiveness. The father joyfully extended his arms to his son and offered him unconditional acceptance. Could you have done that? In all honesty, most people probably would not have met the son halfway. Most people would have greeted their son with a bunch of "I-told-you-so's." Some parents would have said something like, "Yeah, you want to come home, now that your money's run out. Your little so-called friends are gone." Unfortunately, a lot of parents would feel justified in responding this way, and yet wonder why their children do not talk to them.

Just like the father took his son back blamelessly, God will always take you back blamelessly. Someone asked me one day, "Why are you so free with people? Why are you so forgiving? Why do you give people another chance—people that you know have wronged you?" I said, "Because I've been forgiven." When you have been forgiven, you have no right to judge anyone. It does not matter who is right or who is wrong. Just try to stay right.

The Father Took Him Back Bountifully

When the son returned, his father gave him a robe for his body, a ring for his finger, sandals for his feet and a party to celebrate his homecoming. He ordered the fatted calf to be killed for the celebration. The father did not just give his son a place to stay or food to eat. He gave bountifully.

The Father Took Up For Him Boldly

While they were having the party, dancing and having a good time, the older brother got an attitude. When a person comes to the Lord, our heavenly Father throws a party in heaven. If God gives you a party, some people are going to be on the outside complaining about what is going on inside—and they have not even been inside. The Bible says the older brother asked someone else, "What's going on in there?" It would seem that he would have gone inside to check it out for himself. He did not want to celebrate the return of his rebellious brother. He was filled with feelings of jealousy and insecurity. Instead of buying into his older son's insecurity, the father walked out there and straightened him out. His dad said, "It's right for us to party and be excited. It's right for us to celebrate your brother's return. It's right for us to kill the fatted calf, because he was lost and he's now found." Do you know what happened? The brother never said another word.

Many of us cannot deal with criticism. When we hear it we actually leave the party to straighten out the mess. Who left the party to address the criticism? The dad. Let God handle the mess! Let God handle the people who do not like you. Let God handle the people who stare. The son who had returned kept on partying while his father worked out the mess. His mentality was this: "My brother won't come to the party, but that won't stop the party." Just because some people do not like you, that will not stop the blessings of God. God's anointing on your life does not stop just because people do not accept you. Your job is to stay focused on what God has given you. Just keep on partying.

When you look at this story closely, you will discover that both boys were lost. One was lost away from home and the other one was lost at home. You can be lost at church. You can be lost sitting in the pulpit. You can be lost and waving your hands in praise.

Do not let guilt take you under or destroy you. If God has forgiven you, forgive yourself. All of us have done things that other people would be shocked to know. All of us have done things we are not proud of. Even Christians who have lived awhile and have been through some things have come to the point where they no longer say what they will not do. What do seasoned Christians say? "Thank God, He's not done with me yet!" Be careful how you say, "I'll never..." and "I can't believe ... about so-and-so." If you see other parents' kids get pregnant and you start talking about them—watch out! Learn how to pray for people, love them, forgive them and receive them—let God handle all the messiness.

CHAPTER SIX

Winning The Battle Over

HATRED

— Genesis 33 —

O f all the negative emotions we have to overcome in life—guilt, grief, bitterness, worry and a host of other things, perhaps the most menacing is hatred. Genesis 33:1–16 reveals an important truth about dealing with hatred. But before we examine our text, let us look at six biblical facts about hatred.

- Hatred can be sensed.
- Hatred can be between siblings.
- Hatred can be a by-product of sin.
- Hatred can be senseless.
- Hatred cannot be the Spirit.
- Hatred can be in the synagogue.

In Genesis 26:27, Isaac is talking to Abimelech, who had asked to meet with him. Isaac said to him, *"Wherefore come ye to me, seeing ye hate me and have sent me away from you?"* This exchange between the two men suggests that you can sense when people do not like you. You can sense when people harbor hatred in their hearts against you. No matter how they may try to fake, hide or to cover it up, hatred can be sensed.

In Genesis 37, we find Joseph's brothers speaking of hatred. Verse 4 reads, *"And when his brethren saw that their father loved him more than all his brethren, they hated him, and could not speak peaceably unto him."* Hatred can not only be sensed, it can also exist among family members, even between siblings. Joseph could feel his brothers' hatred. Hatred can exist between brothers and sisters in the family, and also between brothers and sisters in the faith.

A third thing we learn about hatred as we study God's Word is found in II Samuel 13:15. Here we find the story of Amnon, who raped his sister Tamar. It says, *"Then Amnon hated her exceedingly so that the hatred wherewith he hated her was greater than the love wherewith he loved her."* Amnon's love turned to hatred after he raped his sister. This suggests that hatred follows sin. Amnon was consumed with desire for his sister, so much so that he raped her. However, after the rape, he hated her. He thought he loved her. He told her that he loved her and could not live without her, but after he got what he wanted, he hated her. Hatred can be sensed, hatred can be between siblings and hatred can be a by-product of sin.

The fourth thing we learn about hatred is in the New Testament. In John 15:25, we discover that even Jesus experienced hatred toward Him: *"But this cometh to pass that the word might be fulfilled, that it is written in their law. They hated me without a cause."* So hatred can be senseless.

People can hate you when it does not make sense. People can hate you and not even know why they hate you. They can hate you without a valid reason for the way they feel.

The fifth biblical fact is that hatred is not of the Spirit. Galatians 5:19–20 addresses the works of the flesh: *"Now the works of the flesh are manifest which are these: Adultery, fornication, uncleanness, lasciviousness, idolatry, witchcraft, hatred..."* Hatred is not spiritual. In other words, God does not lead you to hate people. God does not and will not say, "My will for you is to hate Brother or Sister So-and-So."

An interesting lesson of truth is found in Hosea 9:7–8. Here, God is condemning the nation of Israel—His people:

> *"The days of visitation are come, the days of recompence are come; Israel shall know it: the prophet is a fool, the spiritual man is mad, for the multitude of thine iniquity, and the great hatred. The watchman of Ephraim was with my God: but the prophet is a snare of a fowler in all his ways, and hatred in the house of his God."*

In other words, hatred can be in the synagogue. I am suggesting that a preacher can preach in the pulpit and still hate. A choir member can sing in the choir and still hate. A church member can wave hands of praise and still hate. An usher can stand at the door and still hate. A trustee can work in the parking lot and still hate. You can sit in the pew and say "Amen," and still hate.

The best emotion to live out is love and perhaps the most destructive human emotion is hate. To hate is to detest, loathe or abhor someone or something. A classic biblical example of hatred is the relationship between two brothers, Esau and Jacob. This chapter will examine their lives to show us how to overcome hatred. Thousands of years after these two brothers lived, hatred can still have the same negative effect on us and, thousands of years later, the solution to overcoming hatred remains unchanged.

In order to better comprehend the lesson on hatred in Genesis 33, we have to go back to Genesis 27 to fully understand the relationship between Esau and Jacob. Esau and Jacob were not only brothers, they were fraternal twins. They were born to Isaac and Rebecca. The story of their birth is recorded in Genesis 25. Isaac was 40 years old when he took Rebecca for his wife. Genesis 25:21 says, *"And Isaac entreated the Lord for his wife."* He prayed for Rebecca because she was barren. Look at what happened as a result of his prayer: *"Rebecca his wife conceived" (Gen. 25:21).* Prayer is powerful!

As Rebecca was carrying her sons, the babies struggled in her womb. She asked the Lord,

> *"If it be so, why am I thus? And the Lord said unto her, Two nations are in your womb, and two manner of people shall be separated from thy bowels; and the one people shall be stronger than the other and the elder shall serve the younger" (Gen. 25:22–23).*

If you read the rest of the chapter, you will discover that Esau was born very hairy and Jacob was very smooth. Jacob came out of the womb holding on to his brother's heel. God told Rebecca that the youngest boy would be the leader of the oldest boy.

One day after the brothers had grown up, Esau got so hungry that he gave up his birthright for a bowl of soup. Esau saw his brother making some soup and said to him, "I'm starving. I'm at the point of death." Jacob said, "What are you willing to give me for something to eat?" Esau said "I'll give you my birthright."

The birthright was something long-term. Esau gave up something long-term for something short-term. He gave up something that was lasting for something that was temporary. Sometimes in our impulsiveness, we compromise the eternal to satisfy the flesh. When Esau sold his birthright, he did not think it was a big deal. Like people often do in life, Esau did not think much about his rash decision. It is only later when our choices yield negative consequences, that we consider what we have done.

It was bad enough that Esau had so little regard for his birthright, but he was also the

It is only later when our choices yield negative consequences, that we consider what we have done.

victim of betrayal. His mother and brother plotted to steal his blessing. Genesis 27:1 unfolds the plot of deception and betrayal:

> *"And it came to pass, that when Isaac was old, and his eyes were dim, so that he could not see, he called Esau, his eldest son, and said unto him, My son: and he said unto him, Behold, here am I. And he said, Behold now, I am old, I know not the day of my death: Now therefore take, I pray thee, thy weapons, thy quiver and thy bow, and go out to the field, and take me some venison. And make me savory meat, such as that I love, and bring it to me that I may eat it; that my soul may bless thee before I die" (Gen. 27:1–4).*

Verse 5 reveals that Rebecca overheard Isaac's request: *"And Rebecca heard when Isaac spake to Esau his son. And Esau went to the field to hunt for venison, and to bring it."* How did Rebecca hear? Was she eavesdropping? Rebecca told Jacob what she overheard and gave him the plan:

> *"Now therefore, my son, obey my voice according to that which I command thee. Go now to the flock, and fetch me from thence two good kids of the goats; and I will make them savoury meat for thy father, such as he loveth: And thou shalt bring it to thy father,*

*that he may eat, and that he may bless thee
before his death" (Gen. 27:8–10).*

After hearing the plan, Jacob had only one concern: his
brother was hairy and he was smooth-skinned. Although
Isaac was old and going blind, surely he would be able to
tell the difference between the two sons. Jacob feared that
if Isaac figured it out, *"I shall seem to him as a deceiver;
and I shall bring a curse upon me, and not a blessing"
(Gen. 27:11–12).*

Rebecca told Jacob, "Don't you worry about that. You
just listen to me." Jacob got the meat and Rebecca cooked it
just the way Isaac liked. Then, she got Esau's best clothes
and told Jacob to put them on. Rebecca took the skins of the
young goats and put them on Jacob's hands and neck so he
would feel hairy like his brother. She did all of this to deceive
her husband. She wanted to insure that her youngest son
received the birthright.

Wait! Hadn't God already said that the elder would serve
the younger? Since she knew what God had promised, what
was she guilty of? She was trying to make it happen herself.
Her actions teach us that God can make you a promise and
you can still get out of His will by trying to make it happen
before it is time. That is what Rebecca did. When Jacob
appeared before his father pretending to be Esau, Isaac
asked, "How did you get back so quickly? Jacob replied,
"The Lord blessed me." Isn't it amazing how we sometimes
scheme and have the audacity to blame it on God? Jacob
and Rebecca successfully deceived Isaac and Jacob received

the blessing. Shortly afterward, Esau returned. Isaac said to his oldest son, "I've already given the blessing to your brother. I do not have another one to give." Esau begged his dad, *"Bless me, even me also, O my father" (Gen. 27:34).*

Genesis 27:41 reveals the intense feelings that Esau developed as a result of what happened:

Some people, even Christians, take comfort in killing those who seem to have something to live for.

> *"And Esau hated Jacob because of the blessing wherewith his father blessed him: and Esau said in his heart, The days of mourning for my father are at hand; then will I slay my brother Jacob."*

In other words, Esau was saying, "If it's the last thing I do, I'm going to kill that boy." He hated his brother.

Verse 42 says: *"And these words of Esau her elder son were told to Rebekah."* Their mother had her finger in everything. The verse continues,

> *"She sent and called Jacob her younger son, and said unto him, Behold, thy brother Esau, as*

*touching thee, doth comfort himself, purposing
to kill thee" (Gen. 27:42).*

Rebecca realized that Esau planned to comfort himself by killing his brother. This suggests that some people are comforted by hurting others. Some people in church find comfort in killing others.

What do I mean by killing in the church? Many children of God have had their reputations killed. Some have had their joy for service killed. Others have had their faith murdered. Some people's spirits have been bludgeoned by someone in the church. Some people, even Christians, take comfort in killing those who seem to have something to live for.

Rebecca's scheming continued in verses 43–44. She told Jacob, *"Now therefore, my son, obey my voice; and arise, flee thou to Laban my brother to Haran; And tarry with him a few days, until thy brother's fury turns away."* She thought Esau's anger would die down in a few days. She told Jacob to go to her brother's house for a few days and when Esau's anger had settled down, he could come back home. So Jacob ran. Do you know the last word he heard his brother say as he was running? "I'm going to kill you."

By Chapter 33, twenty years had passed and Jacob was getting ready to go home, but there was one problem—He was still afraid that Esau wanted to kill him. Every time he picked up the telephone, he wondered if it was Esau saying, "I'm going to kill you." Every time he went online and checked his email, he wondered if there was a message from Esau, saying, "You can run, but you cannot hide. And

I am still going to kill you." Jacob lived in fear for twenty years because he thought his brother was still mad enough to kill him.

Despite Jacob's paranoia, so much time had passed since he left that he was returning home a wealthy man. He had two wives, Leah and Rachel, two concubines and eleven children. He also had all kinds of livestock and a whole lot of other things that he did not have when he left. Yet, the thought at the forefront of his mind was: "Esau is going to kill me." Jacob became wealthy while living with his Uncle Laban, but he was also fooled. In Genesis 29:15–28, the schemer was schemed and the trickster was tricked.

Before Jacob returned home, he had an encounter with God in Chapter 32. The Bible says he wrestled with an angel of the Lord and told the angel, *"I will not to let thee go, except thou bless me" (Gen. 32:26).* The Bible says that the angel broke his thigh, which gave him a limp. When you meet God, you should walk differently.

Although Jacob was changed after his encounter with God, he was still scared. So he sent messengers to scout things out. When they returned, they said, "Esau is coming to meet you with four hundred men." This news

When you have not been praying as long as you have been plotting, it is easier to plot than it is to pray.

distressed Jacob to the point that he sent gifts ahead to try to appease Esau.

Look at what happened in Chapter 33, verse 1: *"And Jacob lifted up his eyes, and looked, and, behold, Esau came"*—he was really scared then—and *"with him four hundred men."* Jacob divided the children among Leah, Rachel and the two handmaids. He put the handmaids and their children first, Leah and her children after them, and then Rachel and Joseph in the back. Do you know what he was doing? Scheming. He was thinking, "If Esau is going to kill me, let him kill the women and children I don't care about first." He had met God, but he was still scheming. His actions point out that even after you have met God, if your back is up against the wall, you can fall back on what you know best. When you have not been praying as long as you have been plotting, it is easier to plot than it is to pray. Jacob had been changed, but he was still scheming.

We must stop letting people in the church fool us—just because they have on makeup or the microphone in their hands. Just because they love God, does not mean they are not human. One sentence that every believer should take out of his or her vocabulary is "I'm surprised he did that." Nothing surprises me anymore. If you are a human being, you can mess up. Genesis 33:3 explains that Jacob *"passed over before them and bowed himself to the ground seven times, until he came near his brother."* When he bowed this time, he was not praying. What is he doing? He was trying to say to his brother, "Just forgive me, man. I'm sorry, man.

I did you wrong, man." Every time a man gets on his knees, it is not to pray. Jacob was trying to manipulate Esau. He was conniving to keep his brother from killing him. Jacob was still a trickster.

In verse 4, Esau ran to meet him, embraced him, fell on his neck and kissed him. Both brothers cried. Jacob was probably crying the most. He probably said to himself, "Hallelujah! God is a good God!" In verse 5, Esau lifted his eyes, saw the women and the children, and asked, "Who are these people with you? Jacob said, *"The children which God hath graciously given thy servant (Gen. 33:5).* Jacob called himself Esau's servant.

In verse 6, the handmaids came and bowed down, followed by Leah and her children. Then Joseph and Rachel came near and bowed. Esau asked, "Why did you send me all that stuff?" Jacob said, *"These are to find grace in the sight of my Lord" (Gen. 33:8).* What was he really saying? He was trying to find forgiveness by buying his brother. In verse 9, Esau said, "I have enough, my brother. Keep what you have." Jacob tried to convince his brother to accept his gifts. "No, please!" said Jacob. "If I have found favor in your eyes, accept this gift from me. Seeing your face is like seeing the face of God, now that you have received me favorably. Please accept the present that was brought to you. God has been gracious to me and I have all I need" (Gen. 33:10-11). Because Jacob insisted, Esau accepted.

In verse 12, Esau said, *"Let us take our journey and let us go, and I will go before you."* Jacob explained to his brother that he could not travel quickly because of the young children and livestock. He knew they could not survive a hard journey. Esau offered to leave some of his men behind to help his brother along the journey, and then returned to where he was going. Do you see him getting over hatred?

Overcoming Hatred

By retracing the events of Esau and Jacob's lives, we can understand how we may overcome hatred today. Overcoming hatred involves five actions:

- Pursuing progress
- Refusing revenge
- Forgiving freely
- Accepting apologies
- Parting peaceably

If you are going to overcome hatred, you must do some pursuing, refusing, forgiving, accepting and parting in peace.

1. Pursue Progress

The thing you will have to pursue is progress. It is seen in Genesis 33:4, *"And Esau ran to meet him."* Who hated whom? Esau hated Jacob. Who did who wrong? Jacob did Esau wrong, but in order to overcome his feelings of hatred, Esau had to be willing to pursue progress. He had to be willing to meet his brother and be proactive in restoring the relationship.

If you are going to get over what is bothering you, you cannot lie dormant. You will have to pursue some of the people who bothered you. You will have to pursue some of the people whom you have bad feelings against. The reason why many people cannot get over their feelings of hatred, strife and envy is because they are waiting for the person who did them wrong to do something to make them feel better.

Why should you do the pursuing, if you were the one wronged? Because you are the one harboring the feelings of hatred.

Why should you do the pursuing, if you were the one wronged? Because *you* are the one harboring the feelings of hatred. You are the one who cannot sleep at night. You are the one who has an ulcer. You are the one who has gallstones. If you are the one who cannot get over it, you have to pursue progress.

Hatred will paralyze you. Hatred will stop you from moving. Hatred will get you to the point where you do not even want to do what is right. Let me give you an example: Some church members can have bad feelings about other church members. Yet, they come to church to praise God and give Him glory. Although they are coming to church to do something good, their hatred is affecting them. When they see the person for whom they have bad feelings, they forget all about saying "Amen." They forget all about lifting holy hands. All of a sudden, the spirit of praise leaves them. If the person they hate could take their spirit, they did not have the right spirit in the first place.

If someone can take your joy, you did not have it in the first place. You have to let people know, "I'm not going to let you take my joy. I'm not going to let you take my shout. I'm not going to let you take my praise for God. I'll praise God with you sitting right next to me, because you didn't put a roof over my head. You didn't keep clothes on my back. I know where my help comes from."

Whenever you get to the point where people bother you so much that you cannot sit by them in church, ride with them on the church bus or serve in the same ministry with them, then something is wrong with *your* heart.

I go to church to glorify God. I do not go to make friends. I go to fulfill the kingdom's agenda. I am pursuing progress. You have to reach a point where you say, "I can't live like this. I can't work like this. I can't serve like this. I have to get this hatred out of me."

Hatred will get you to the point where you do not even want to do what is right.

Pursuing progress toward reconciliation and away from hatred is not about the other person. It is about you. It is not about what they did. It's about what you are going to do to get over it. Despite what he had done, Esau ran to meet Jacob, the brother who wronged him. If you are waiting on the person who wronged you to come to you, then you have a problem. Even if they come, you still will not get over it because once they come, you will change the issue by saying, "What took you so long to come to me?"

2. Refuse Revenge

Esau refused to embrace revenge. He embraced Jacob, fell on his neck, kissed him and then they cried together. You must get to the point in your life where you refuse to take revenge on people who have done you wrong. You have to refuse revenge and say, "I refuse to be pulled down to that level. I refuse to lower myself by showing out on you. Not that I don't have a good reason to, but I refuse. I refuse to go crazy. I refuse to stoop down. I refuse to let a demon use me. I refuse to let hell come out of me." When anger and hatred are in you, then you have to do battle with *yourself*. Some saints talk about doing battle with the devil, but in reality, you need to learn to handle yourself. How can you do battle with principalities and powers when you can't even handle yourself?

All of us have been offended by someone, but we must refuse revenge. Someone will always say something to cross you. There is always someone out there who is willing to betray you. There are plenty of people out there who will try to use you. They are out there, and if you are not careful, you will be used. You will be a lot better off if you refuse to indulge in revenge.

I had a personal challenge with refusing revenge when a member of my church crossed me the wrong way. I should have refused revenge, but I couldn't help it. We were talking on the phone and she was sharing some of her concerns. We were having a good conversation, and then she said, "I want to compliment you, Pastor. You have become very kind. You have become very loving and joyous. You've become real nice. You were not always like that." I had never had anyone say anything like that to me! I had never heard anyone accuse me of being moody. I had never heard anyone say I was unkind. I had never been accused of being unloving, or lacking patience or not being longsuffering. When she said those things, I knew that I should have just taken the compliment and moved on, but I was not feeling strong that day. She closed the conversation by saying, "I don't know what happened, but I'm glad to see the change." I should have just hung up, but I said, "I'll tell you what happened, you probably changed. You probably see things differently now. The problem was not in me." I should have refused, but being human, I don't always refuse revenge either. I felt badly afterward and wished I had refused revenge.

3. Forgive Freely

Not only must we pursue progress and refuse revenge, but we must also forgive freely. In Genesis 33:9, Esau told Jacob, "I have enough, man. You don't have to buy me. I have enough." When you forgive, it enables you to release some things. Some people cannot forgive freely. Others will not forgive until the person ingratiates himself—takes you out and buys your lunch. Some of you believe that in order to let it go, you have to feel as though you have literally gotten back everything that was taken from you. Until you get it back, you will have a problem forgiving. The person can say, "I'm sorry" all he wants, but until you get that money back, there is no forgiveness. The person can say "I love you," but until she brings that hat back or until he brings that tie back, you will not let it go. Everytime you see them, you are looking to see if they have what they took from you. They can owe you as little as five dollars and you cannot sleep at night—over five dollars. Whatever it is, you have to let it go. I am not saying you should not want what was taken from you, but when you forgive freely, you are still okay, even if you do not get it back. Why should you forgive freely? Because God will

God will never let anything be taken from you without bringing something back to you.

never let anything be taken from you without bringing something back to you.

4. Accept Apologies

In Genesis 33:11, Jacob said, "Take it, man. Take it." He wanted his brother to take the gifts because that was Jacob's way of knowing that Esau had freely forgiven him and accepted his apology. It is not enough for people to say, "I'm sorry." You have to accept their apology.

Make a conscious effort to check yourself when someone comes to you and says, "I'm sorry. Will you accept my apology?" Make sure you can say, "Yes." Many times people will say, "I'm sorry," instead of "Will you accept my apology?" because many of us are not mature in the Lord. When someone says, "I'm sorry. Will you accept my apology?" it forces the other person to check his or her response.

When asked, "Will you accept my apology?" most people do not respond because they want to reserve the right to get mad again. We want to reserve the right to bring up the hurt at our convenience, but when you tell someone "I accept your apology," that means you have to let it go. You will always have people who want to relive the past and remind you and others of what your life used to be like. For example, someone could say, "You know, I thank God for Sister Martha, when she leads praise and worship, it's a real blessing to me. I get so much out of it. I'm so glad she's not like she used to be." They are ready to bring up negative issues from your past that have nothing to do with anything.

5. Part Peaceably

Verse 16 says that Esau returned that day. When Esau left, he did not leave grumbling. You can pursue progress, refuse revenge, forgive freely and accept the apology, but if you do not part peaceably, you still have issues. It is not over because nothing has been resolved until you can part peaceably. After saying what you have to say, and hearing what you have to hear, you must be able to turn and walk away peaceably. What cripples many people is they communicate better with the people who are not involved in the situation than with those with whom they are upset. You have to learn to let go of the anger. Why? Because if you do not let it go, it will come back at the wrong time.

Allow me to give you a biblical example: When Joseph's brothers were reunited with him years later, they said, "We're sorry. We'll be your servants." Joseph said, *"Ye thought evil against me, but God meant it for good" (Gen. 50:20).* He said, "I'm in this place because of what you did, but if you hadn't done it, I wouldn't be where I am." Joseph showed them that he had no hard feelings toward them when he invited them to live in Egypt. He said, "I'm going to take care of you and your children." After they had moved there and their father died, the brothers came together and talked. They were afraid that Joseph would seek revenge now that their father was dead. Joseph had forgiven them, but they had not forgiven themselves.

When you do not forgive yourself, you will carry the past with you into every relationship you have. A wife may seek counseling about her husband, but the problem is not her husband. The problem is the man whom she was with previously. Because she did not deal with the issues she had with the previous man, she takes it out on her husband. The problem with many fathers and their children is the way they were treated by their fathers. They have issues with their children because they never dealt with the pain their fathers put them through.

Maybe you never dealt with your mother not saying "I love you," and now you take it out on everyone who tries to show you love because you never let go of those negative feelings. So you come to church and want to shout out your pain, but you cannot shout out everything. You may come to church because you want to worship it out, but you cannot worship out everything.

Some issues must be dealt with head on. Some issues just have to be faced. If it takes counseling, then get counseling. If it takes reading, then buy some books. If it takes lying before the Lord, then lie before God. The important thing is to deal with it before you destroy everything you put your hands on. When you let go of that thing, even when people bring it up again, you can say like

Whatever your issue is, let it go right now because you need to be able to shout, "I'm free!"

Joseph, "I told you what you meant for evil twenty years ago, God meant it for good. I'm not mad at you. If it hadn't been for you, I wouldn't be where I am."

Whatever your issue is, let it go right now because you need to be able to shout, "I'm free!" When you are free, you can sleep at night. When you are free, you do not have time to sweat over small stuff. When you are free, you do not have time to chase people down running after lies and gossip, trying to defend yourself. When you are free, you can say, "If you don't like me, that's your problem."

Do you know where that freedom starts? In your mind, that's where! That is what the battle is for—your mind. The battle of the mind is important because whoever controls your mind, controls you. Philippians 2:5 reads, *"Let this mind be in you which was also in Christ Jesus."*

My grandmother used to sing, "I woke up this morning with my mind stayed on Jesus." Why did our elders know that it was important to wake up with their minds on Jesus? Why are we still learning today that there "Ain't no harm to keep your mind stayed on Jesus"? The reason is because you cannot keep your mind on Jesus and mess at the same time. You cannot pray in the Spirit and cuss in the flesh at the same time.

Isaiah 26:3 reads, *"Thou wilt keep him in perfect peace whose his mind is stayed on thee."* Do not allow hatred to eat away at your happiness and peace of mind. The person you have issues with may not even know it or care. Let go of hatred for your own sake.

CHAPTER SEVEN

Winning The Battle Over
JEALOUSY

— I Samuel 26 —

In the 31 chapters of the Book of I Samuel, there are three major characters—Samuel, Saul and David. In the first eight chapters, Samuel is at the forefront. In Chapters 9–15, Saul who was anointed by Samuel as the first king of Israel, is featured prominently. David, who also was anointed by Samuel as king of Israel, is featured in Chapters 16–31. Samuel had the blessed opportunity to anoint both Saul and David. However, when Samuel anointed David, Saul was still king, which suggests that sometimes God will anoint you for something even while someone else has it.

Although someone may have power, position, wealth, good looks, intelligence or some other asset or virtue, it does not guarantee that the person will not harbor feelings of jealousy. Saul was king, but he was jealous of David, a shepherd boy. Unfortunately, no matter how gifted or blessed a person may be, it does not prevent the jealousy demon from entering the person's heart. Jealousy is a negative emotion that is even found within the body of Christ.

First Samuel 26 opens with David and King Saul in a meeting. David asked:

> *"Wherefore doth my lord thus pursue after his servant? For what have I done? Or what evil is in mine hand? Now therefore, I pray thee, let my lord the king hear the words of his servant. If the Lord have stirred thee up against me, let him accept an offering; but if they be the children of men, cursed be they before the Lord; for they have driven me out this day from abiding in the inheritance of the Lord, saying, Go, serve other gods. Now therefore let not my blood fall to the earth before the face of the Lord, for the king is of Israel, Israel is come out to see a flea as when one doth hunt a partridge in the mountains. Then said Saul, I have sinned, return my son David for I will no more do thee harm because my soul was precious in thine eyes, this day, behold I have played the fool and have erred exceedingly"* (I Sam. 26:18–21).

In order to understand David and Saul's relationship, it would be wise to start reading in I Samuel 16 and 17. In I Samuel 16, David is anointed to become the next king of Israel. In Chapter 17, he meets his adversary, Goliath. For every anointing there is an adversary.

What sometimes hinders us is that we always want the Chapter 16 experience, the anointing, but we do not want to deal with the Chapter 17 experience—the adversary. After David's anointing and meeting his adversary, he experiences advancement. In Chapter 18, David moved into the palace to work under King Saul. He advanced from a shepherd boy to living and working in the king's palace. The biblical record of David's adventure appears in Chapter 19 through the end of the book. In these chapters, David is on the run. Why would a man who was living in the palace and working directly with the king be on the run? He was running because he had encountered a demon-possessed, jealous man named Saul.

Chapter 18 explains that Saul had become consumed with jealousy. He was not just jealous, he was consumed with jealousy. Here is what happened: David had just finished killing Goliath in Chapter 17. In Chapter 18, Saul heard the words to a song that disturbed him. The song, said: *"Saul has killed a thousand, but David has killed ten thousand" (I Sam. 18:7).* Those words caused Saul to be filled with jealousy. He was so consumed with jealousy that he said, "If it's the last thing I do, I'm going to kill David."

Chapter 18 reveals five things that made Saul jealous of David. It is important to know what they are because the same things that made Saul jealous of David are the same kinds of thoughts that make us jealous today.

First, Saul was jealous of **David's performance**. In I Samuel 18:6, David killed Goliath, and Saul did not like that. Before David killed Goliath, Saul had a chance to fight

Goliath, but he was scared and weak so he refused to fight. Then, David killed Goliath and Saul got jealous. Isn't it amazing that we get mad with people over their accomplishments although we had a chance to do it first?

Saul was not only jealous over David's performance, he was also jealous over **David's praise.** After David's victory against Goliath, the women sang *"Saul has killed a thousand, but David has killed ten thousand" (I Sam. 18:7).* Saul was alright with the first line of the song, but it was the second line that messed him up. Many times, we cannot take someone getting more praise than us. We are alright as long as we think we are the top dog and everybody is saying how great we are. We are alright as long as we are the ones "living large and in charge," but as soon as someone else moves up the ladder, we cannot take it.

The third thing that made Saul jealous was **David's position.** Verse 16 says that the people began to treat David as one of them. They treated David as if he had grown up with them. They treated David as if he were a "homey" from the hood, a person they had known all of their lives.

How often do people get jealous over someone being promoted to supervisor? How

Many times, we cannot take someone getting more praise than us.

often do we see people get jealous because someone moved from an apartment to a house or from a Ford to Lexus? How often do other people become jealous when someone moves from singlehood to marriage?

The fourth thing Saul got jealous over was **David's power**. In I Samuel 18:12, Saul noticed that the Lord was with David. Saul did not like it, but he knew God was with young David. Saul could not stand David, but he knew God was with him. He wanted to kill David, but he knew God was with him. Even the people who do not like you should see God in you. Even the people who do not want to be around you should see God's anointing upon you. Other people should be able to say, "God is with you."

Finally, Saul was jealous because of **David's popularity**. All of the people began to fall in love with David (I Sam. 18:16). They thought David was great and wanted to be around him. The people were singing David's praises and Saul could not take losing the spotlight. So Saul said, "I'm going to kill him. I have to kill him."

Is there any Saul in you? Truthfully, there is a little Saul in all of us. The real question is: How much? All of us get jealous over something, but how much? In Chapter 18, David was working in the king's palace when Saul made up his mind, "I'm just going to take my spear and kill him" (I Sam. 18:11). Several opportunities came where Saul just threw his spear. Finally, David said, "I have to get out of here" (I Sam. 19:12).

It is alright to be anointed and have common sense. Some people think that because you are anointed, you cannot be logical, but David was wise enough to know that although he was anointed, he did not need to be on a job where his boss was trying to kill him everyday.

David had a covenant relationship with Jonathan, Saul's son. They were best friends. David ran to Jonathan and asked, "What have I done that was so bad that your daddy is trying to kill me?" (I Sam. 20:1). Jonathan said, "No, my dad's not like that. He's not going to do you any harm. Let me go talk to him about you. I'll find out what he's thinking and then I'll come back and let you know" (I Sam. 20:2).

When Jonathan talked to his dad in Chapter 20, he said, "Dad, what do you have against David? He's never done you any wrong, Dad. Why are you trying to do harm to him?" When Jonathan said that, Saul's anger and jealousy rose to the point that he took a spear and tried to kill his own son. When Jonathan saw that spear coming at him, he ran after David and said, "You're right, man. You need to get out of here. There's something wrong with my dad." After this confirmation from Jonathan, David went on the run from Saul. While David was on the run, Saul had several opportunities to meet with David and overcome his jealousy. The first meeting is recorded in Chapter 24 and the second is in Chapter 26.

You Can Overcome Jealousy

There are three things you can do to overcome feelings of jealousy.

1. Stop Patronizing the Flesh

The root word of patronizing is *patron.* When you patronize something, you become a consumer of it, one of its regular customers. You may have noticed a sign in some businesses that reads, "Thank you for your patronage." When people start businesses, often they will ask, "Will you patronize me?" You will always get in trouble when you become a customer, client, consumer or buyer to your flesh because your flesh is all about pleasing self.

The flesh says, "Please me." It has a motto and you have heard it before. It is the same as Burger King's slogan, "Have it your way." That is all the flesh is about. Let me help you understand. The last time you cussed someone out—that was for your flesh. The last drink of liquor you had—that was for your flesh. The last time you went on the Internet looking at pornography, you were patronizing your flesh. The last time you committed adultery or fornication—that was for your flesh.

Romans 7 tells us something about the flesh. Paul says, "Every time I try to do something good, evil is present on every hand and I find myself doing what I said I wasn't going to do. I find myself going where I said I

You will always get in trouble when you become a customer, client, consumer or buyer to your flesh because your flesh is all about pleasing self.

wasn't going to go. I find myself saying what I said I wasn't going to say" (Rom. 7:15–21). The flesh will destroy you. Your flesh will keep you trapped in negative emotions. You need to know that as a human being, you are a trichotomy. That means you are a three-part being. You are a spirit, you have a soul, and you live in a body. Your body wants to take your soul away from the spiritual things of God. It is your flesh that says, "Party over here...cocaine over there...smoke over here...sex over there...drugs over here...wild things over there."

Despite his evil intentions, Saul must be given credit for recognizing what he was doing. His actions were not of the Spirit, but of the flesh. In I Samuel 26:21 he says: *"I have sinned."* Sometimes people do not realize that you can preach the Gospel and still be in the flesh. You can sing in the choir and still be in the flesh. You can usher and still be in the flesh. You can lead worship and still be in the flesh. You can sit in church every Sunday and still be in the flesh. Be careful how you patronize your flesh.

2. Stop Pursuing Fleas

In I Samuel 26:20, David said to Saul, *"Why is the king of Israel come out to seek a flea?"* Do you know what David was saying? David was saying "Saul, you're the king. As the king, you are responsible for two million people and a billion-dollar budget. You have 100,000 soldiers who are all accountable to you. You are responsible for insuring that we are governed and doing things the right way. Instead, you're wasting all of your kingly time chasing a flea." David was not talking about a dog or a cat. He was not talking about an animal or insect at all. David was saying to Saul, "When you add up all you're missing to chase me, what you're going after is a flea."

There is a story about a preacher who had his doctoral degree. One day, Dr. Johnson went to his office to get some work done because he had a lot of work to do. There Dr. Johnson was with his earned doctorate going to his office to get some work done. When he walked into his office, he saw a fly, and made up his mind he had to kill this fly. Four hours later, after he had broken his coffeepot, knocked all the pictures off the wall, scattered all the papers on his desk, broken his big toe and sprained his wrist, he caught the fly.

Sometimes we are guilty of expending a lot of effort to chase nothing more than fleas and flies. If you are worried because someone does not speak to you, you are chasing a flea. If someone took your parking spot at the mall and you are yelling and screaming that you were there first, you are chasing a flea! How many times do we fight over an issue that is nothing but a flea? How many times do husbands get into arguments with their wives and sleep on the couch over a flea? How many people have gone to jail over fleas? How many have lost their families over fleas? Who has worried about something so minute, so trivial, only to realize that it was nothing but a flea?

I once heard a story about two boys who went to school together from fourth through twelfth grade. They were best friends, but they lost contact after college. One moved to Arizona, and the other moved to New York. After twenty-five years, they found each other and decided to get together. The one in Arizona was going to visit the one in New York. In order to get there, he had to take a plane. After the plane, he had to take a bus ride. After the bus ride, he had to get on a small ferry. After the ferry, he had to walk through some sand to get to his friend's house in New York. Finally, the day came for the two friends to visit one another. The friend in New York waited and waited and waited for the friend from Arizona to arrive. After waiting for an extremely long time, he finally got a call from his friend. The Arizonan said, "The journey is just too tough. I can't make it." The New Yorker replied, "I understand it is a long plane ride. I understand it is a long bus ride. I understand it is a long boat ride. I understand it's tough to get here." The friend from Arizona said, "Yeah, but it wasn't the plane that turned me around. The bus ride didn't turn me around. It wasn't even the boat ride that turned me around." He said, "What turned me around is I couldn't take the sand getting in my shoes."

So many people can handle the major things in life, but the small stuff, the fleas, turns them upside down and all around. There is a great book by Richard Carlson entitled, *Don't Sweat the Small Stuff* (Hyperion Books: New York, 1997), which shows that much of what we encounter in life is small stuff.

3. Stop Playing the Fool

Saul realized in I Samuel 26:21, *"I have played the fool."* He admitted he had been a fool. There was a song out in the mid-70s by a group called the Main Ingredient that went like this:

> "Everybody plays the fool,
> sometimes.
> No exception to the rule.
> May be factual, may be cruel,
> (I ain't lying) Everybody plays
> the fool."

Psalm 14:1 says, *"The fool has said in his heart there is no God."* How do you know when you are playing the fool? Whenever you try to do things without God's help, you are playing the fool. Saul admitted that God was nowhere in what he was doing. He said, *"I have played the fool and have erred exceedingly" (I Sam. 26:21).* In other words, he said, "I messed up big time."

Are you in a foolish relationship? Are you trying to get a job and have not prayed about it? Are you trying to marry someone who is not saved? In what area of your life are you playing the fool? The apostle Paul called himself a fool for Christ in I Corinthians 4:10.

Whenever you try to do things without God's help, you are playing the fool.

So the question is: Since everybody has to be a fool, whose fool are you?

Whenever you get to a point in your life where nothing is working, it might be because you are being a fool. Whenever everything you touch backfires on you or leads to shame or embarrassment, and you always come out looking all messed up, it might be because you are doing something foolish. You will never get over jealousy by being foolish.

Do you want to know how to stop playing the fool? You must stop pursuing fleas. Why couldn't Saul do that? Because he kept patronizing his flesh. Whenever flesh is your main priority, Satan will always control you.

There was a little boy in the eighth grade who got in trouble at school. His dad was a preacher. He was always messing up at school and at home. Well, he had gotten in trouble once again. That evening at home, his dad looked at him and asked, "Why didn't you tell Satan to get behind you? That's what you should have done. You should have told Satan to get behind you." The boy blew his dad away when he said, "I did tell Satan to get behind me." The dad replied, "If you told Satan to get behind you, how did you get in trouble again?" He said, "When I told Satan to get behind me, Satan said 'Okay. It doesn't matter if I'm behind you or in front of you, because if we're going in the same direction, you're going to do what I want you to do whether I'm pushing you from behind or pulling you from the front!" Sometimes we need to change directions.

I once read a book that was only five chapters long. Chapter 1 said, "I was walking down a street one day and there was a big hole and I fell into it. I didn't see it. It took me forever to get out of it. It wasn't my fault, it was dark. I was scared and it took forever to get out, but I got out." Chapter 2 read, "I was walking down the same street one day, there was a big hole. I saw it this time, but I still fell in. It wasn't as dark, it wasn't as scary, and it didn't take me as long to get out." Chapter 3: "I was walking down the same street one day, and there was that big hole and I fell right in. It's a habit now. That's just what I do. I'm not afraid, I'm not scared, and it takes me no time to get out." Then in Chapter 4: "I was walking down the same street one day, there was that big hole again. I walked around it and I didn't fall. Chapter 5: "I walked down a different street."

No matter who you are, your life is in one of those chapters. Some people are still in Chapter 1—things just keep happening to them. They do not see it, it just keeps happening. They keep getting fired, keep getting pregnant, keep losing this or that—it just happens. Other people are in Chapter 2. They see the hole, but they fall in anyway. It does not blindside them because they see it coming. They just fail to get out of the way. For the people in Chapter 3, falling in the hole is just a habit: "I just spent all of my paycheck on drugs—that's my habit...I just go to happy hour every Friday and come home unhappy. It's just a habit...I just cuss like this. My mother cussed, my father cussed. I just cuss like this when someone gets on my nerves. It's just a habit...My grandmother had a child out of wedlock. My mother had a child out of wedlock. I've had three out of wedlock and I haven't stopped yet. It's just a habit." People living in Chapter 4, see things but they are always trying to walk around them. Nobody is that strong. If you keep walking next to holes, sooner or later you are going to fall in.

Your deliverance, breakthrough, anointing and miracle will only come after you stop making the same mistakes.

Your deliverance, breakthrough, anointing and miracle will only come after you stop making the same mistakes. You will not go to another level unless you stop doing the same foolish things. When you start walking down a different street, you will get power. You will get victory. God will raise you up. Your finances will get better and your marriage will get better.

Sometimes a different street means telling some friends that you cannot talk to them anymore. Sometimes a different street means turning off the television. Sometimes a different street means turning off the negative music because when those lyrics get into your spirit, you start singing and doing things you never thought you would do.

Do you know what I found out? I discovered that God will never take you down a road where He does not have other people there to meet you. Our problem is that we get so stuck on certain people that we do not want to break away. We are scared that if we break away, we will not have anyone to run with, but when you start running with God and walking by faith, God has other people up the road.

Remember Saul confessed, "I messed up." He had already told David, "I'm not going to harm you. Go on your way" (I Sam. 26:21). But two chapters later, it hits him again. In I Samuel 28, Saul learned that the Philistines were coming to kill his entire army. So he went to God and prayed. He asked God to send a prophet, but God refused to answer him because it took him too long to change. I am afraid of God cutting me off. You ought to be afraid that if you do not change, you may reach a point when you desperately need God, and He will cut you off.

Since God had cut him off, Saul decided to check out the psychic hotline. He put on a disguise and went to see a psychic. He told her, "I need you to pull up someone from the dead because I need a word from God" (I Sam. 28:11).

Samuel had died by this time and Saul found himself longing for Samuel's advice. The woman answered, "I can't pull him up, because Saul made a law saying that he would kill anyone who called up someone from the dead" (I Sam. 28:9). He said, "Forget about that law, I swear to God nothing will happen to you because of this" (I Sam. 28":10). God let Samuel come back from the dead. When Samuel started talking, the psychic recognized Saul and got scared.

Samuel told Saul "God has shut you off. You might as well get ready, Brother, because you and your kingdom are going down. You had chance after chance, but you never changed" (I Sam. 28:11–19).

Make up your mind that you do not want God to shut you off because there will come a time when He will get sick and tired of your mess. God is a forgiving God. He's a loving God, but there will come a time when He will say, "Alright, that's enough!"

Saul missed his opportunity for change because he was stuck in a spirit of jealousy. What are you jealous about? Whatever it is, it is not worth it. Let it go!

CHAPTER EIGHT

Winning The Battle Over
WORRY

— Matthew 6:24–34 —

I n the Gospel of Matthew 6:25–34, after addressing a number of other issues in the Sermon on the Mount, Jesus turns to the problem of worry. The Latin word for worry means "to strangle." What does that say that worry will do to you? Worry will choke the life right out of you. It will have you walking around dead while you are still alive. There are some things worry will take out of you, like health, strength and vitality. Worry will also rob you of joy, peace, contentment and a lot of other positive experiences. Jesus warns us in these verses:

> "No man can serve two masters: for either he will hate the one, and love the other: or else he will hold to the one, and despise the other. Ye cannot serve God and mammon. Therefore I say unto you, Take no thought for your life, what ye shall eat, or what ye shall drink; nor yet for your body, what ye shall put on....Take therefore no thought for the morrow: for the

morrow shall take thought for the things of itself. Sufficient unto the day is the evil thereof" (Matt. 6:24–25, 34).

The New Living Bible states the matter a bit differently:

"No one can serve two masters. For you will hate one and love the other or be devoted to one and despise the other. You cannot serve both God and money. So I tell you, don't worry about everyday life—whether you have enough food, drink or clothes. Doesn't life consist of more than food and clothing? Look at the birds. They don't need to plant or harvest or put food in barns because your heavenly Father feeds them. And you are far more valuable to him than they are. Can all your worries add a single moment to your life? Of course not...So don't worry about tomorrow, for tomorrow will bring its own worries. Today's trouble is enough for today" (Matt. 6:24-27, 34 NLT).

It makes no sense to worry about tomorrow, there are enough trials to go through today so you do not need to worry about tomorrow.

What's Wrong With Worrying?

I want to give you some principles that Matthew 6 reveals about worry, and then I want to share what Jesus says

human beings worry about. Finally, I will suggest some ways we can overcome worry.

Worrying is a Sin

We get it straight from the Master's
mouth—worrying is sin. How do we know it is
a sin? We know because in Matthew 6:25, God
tells us not to worry. Whenever you find yourself doing what God told you not to do, you
are sinning. We have to get away from thinking that sin is just doing things like smoking,
drinking and fornicating. There is much more
to sin than that.

Worrying is Not Satisfying

In verse 27 Jesus asked, *"Which of you by
taking thought can add one cubic unto his
stature?"* In other words, he said, "When you
worry, it does not help you one bit." Worrying
never makes things go away, nor does it ease
your mind.

Worrying is Senseless

It is not wise to worry. Look at what Jesus
said in Matthew 6:28–29:

> *"And why do you take thought
> for raiment? Consider the lilies
> of the field, how they grow; they*

If God takes care of birds and flowers, why do you think He will not take care of you?

toil not, neither do they spin: And yet I say unto you, That even Solomon in all his glory was not arrayed like one of these."

Jesus is telling us that worrying is senseless because even the birds do not worry. It is senseless because even the flowers do not worry. If God takes care of birds and flowers, why do you think He will not take care of you? Therefore, Jesus says worry is senseless.

Worrying Is Not for Saints

Jesus says, *"For after all these things do the Gentiles seek" (Matt. 6:32).* (Some translations use the word heathens instead of Gentiles.) In other words, these are the kind of things that unbelievers seek, which suggests that you should not worry about these things, if you are a child of God. Why would you go to church, pay your tithe, read your Bible, pray and worry while worldly people who are caught up in all kinds of wrongdoing sleep well at night? Something is wrong with that picture. Jesus was saying that if anyone is worried, it ought to be the people who do not believe in God. There is no need for you to profess belief in God and worry too.

There is no need for you to profess belief in God and worry too.

Worrying is Selective

No one makes you worry. No one can force you to worry. No one holds a gun to your head and says, "Now worry." You choose to worry. In Matthew 7:25, Jesus says, *"Therefore I say unto you, you take no thought,"* which means it is your decision to worry or not. Then Jesus talked about five things that we tend to worry about.

First, he said we worry about **finances** (Matt. 6:24). We always worry about money. We always worry about how the bills are going to get paid. We always worry about when we are going to get promoted or if we are going to get fired. We are openly consumed with finances, but Jesus tells us that we cannot serve God and money.

Secondly, he said we worry about **food** (Matt. 6:25, 31). He said the birds do not plant or reap, yet God feeds them. Are you not better than the birds? Do you not think that God will feed you?

Thirdly, he said we worry about the **future** (Matt. 6:25). Some of you have your life already mapped out. You may be thirty-two years old and have your life all mapped out. When your life does not go according to what you have on paper, you worry.

Fourthly, he said we worry about **fitness** (Matt. 6:25, 27). You cannot get your hair back by worrying about it. You cannot lose weight by worrying about it. We are overly concerned with fitness. We take pills, we work out, we watch what we eat, and do you know what? We are discovering that everything kills. As soon as you find something that they say is good for you, someone else comes up with something saying it is not good for you.

Finally, he said we worry about **fashion** (Matt. 6:25, 28). Interestingly, Jesus devoted five verses to our worrying about clothes. He talked about how good the lilies look because God clothed them. Even Solomon, the richest, wisest man in the world could not compare to the lilies in their splendor. Why did Jesus spend so much time talking about fashion? He did it because we are always worrying about the next sale. We are always worrying about what we wore last week. We are overly concerned with our wardrobes because we have learned that clothes can cover you. We have learned clothes can hide issues. Clothes not only hide physical imperfections, they also hide emotional and spiritual issues like guilt, pain and stress. What did Adam and Eve do when they felt guilty about sinning? They covered themselves with fig leaves. Many people turn to shopping when they are not feeling their best.

To win the battle over worry, you have to seek God.

Five Steps to Overcoming Worry

Several years ago, Bobby McFerrin had a hit song called "Don't Worry, Be Happy." The message of the song was that people should put their energy into their happiness rather than their anxieties. How can this be done? There are five things that can help anyone overcome worry and anxiety.

1. Seek the Lord

To win the battle over worry, you have to seek God. When you find yourself caught in worry, seek God. Don't seek Him when you have finished worrying. Don't find Him after the worrying is over. Find Him when you are worried. What hinders us from overcoming worry is our tendency to pursue everybody but God. In Matthew 6:33, Jesus says, *"Seek ye first the kingdom of God, and his righteousness; and all these things shall be added unto you."* So many people want to seek the things of the world first, and then seek God. But Jesus said that it does not work that way. Seek God, and then you will get the other things. Who are you seeking? Who are you going after? Who are you pursuing? Who are you running down? Who are you chasing? Seek God when you are worried.

Luke 10 features the story of Mary and Martha, the sisters of Lazarus. Beginning at verse 38 it says:

> *"Now it came to pass that as they went that he entered into a certain village and a certain woman named Martha received him into her house. Martha invited the Savior into her house. And she had a sister called Mary, which also sat at Jesus' feet and heard His words. But Martha was cumbered about much serving, and came to him and said,*

> *Lord, dost thou not care that my sister hath*
> *left me to serve alone? bid her therefore that*
> *she help me. And Jesus answered and said*
> *unto her, Martha, Martha, thou art careful*
> *and troubled about many things: But one*
> *thing is needful: and Mary hath chosen that*
> *good part, which shall not be taken away*
> *from her"* (Luke 10:40–42).

Jesus came over for dinner and, as soon as he got in the house, Mary fell at His feet to hear His word. Meanwhile, Martha was worried about the meal. She got so worked up about it that she said to Jesus, "Make Mary worry about what I'm worried about." Isn't it amazing that when people are worried, they do not want to worry alone? Even in church, people want you to make their priority your priority. Martha tried to get Jesus to help her get someone to be worried with her. She tried to make Him do what was important to her. Jesus quickly said to her, "Martha, you're worried about the wrong thing. Only one thing is needful and Mary has chosen the best part." Replace your worry with the Word of God. Make an exchange and give up your worry. His Word is the only thing needful.

2. Stand On God's Word

There is a story about a time when the Green Bay Packers were going through training camp and they had to reduce the team to fifty-three players. So, they started cutting. Generally, when they cut a player, the first thing they will do is tell him, "Turn in your playbook" because they do not want him to get picked up by another team and share their playbook with someone else. With about two playoff games left, they called one player into the office and told him, "Bring your playbook." That's all they said. The player decided, "They won't cut me like this. They're not rejecting me like this." So he packed his clothes, got in his car, and drove down the highway headed home. Two hours later the team's management called him on his mobile phone and asked him, "Why did you leave?" He answered, "I couldn't take the rejection. I couldn't take you cutting me like that." They said to him, "We weren't cutting you." Curious, he asked, "Then why did you ask for my playbook?" They explained, "Because we wanted to add some plays, so come on back." He went back. They added the plays. He stayed about a week, and then they cut him for foolish behavior.

Sometimes we get messed up, not by what someone has said, but how we interpret what they said. If the doctor's office says "Come in for another checkup," you might assume that it is cancer. If the boss says, "I need to see you first thing in the morning," you cannot sleep the rest of the night. Don't assume. Stand on God's Word.

3. Speak to God About Your Worries

Philippians 4:6 reads, *"Be careful for nothing; but in every thing by prayer"*. In this verse, Paul is really saying, "Don't worry about anything." *Be careful* means "worry." What messes people up is praying about nothing and worrying about everything. The Bible says to worry about nothing, but pray about everything.

Let me help you understand the difference between seeking the Lord and speaking to God about your worries. Step one is seeking, but step three is speaking. Just because you are seeking, does not mean you are speaking. Just because you find God, does not mean you talk to Him. Some people seek God by going to church every Sunday, but they do not have prayer time at home so they are not speaking to God. Some people seek God by going to Bible study, but they do not talk to God about helping them apply what they learn to everyday life so there is no speaking. It is not enough to seek God. You must speak to Him, too. You have to grow to where you pray about everything—your in-laws, the mortgage, the gas bill, friends, family—everything.

The Bible says to worry about nothing, but pray about everything.

4. Thankfully Share With God

The fourth step is also recorded in Philippians 4:6: *"But in everything prayer and supplication with thanksgiving."* The word supplication means to pray specifically. The time is going to come when a general prayer will not be enough. You may not have time to say, "The God of Abraham, the God of Isaac, the God of Jacob, thank You for last night's laying down, and an early morning rising. Thank You that my bed wasn't my cooling board." The time is going to come when your back is against the wall and you have to get right to the issue, "God I need this job and I need it now." "God, I need You to touch my child right now." Paul is saying, "Pray specifically, and with thanksgiving."

Even when you are worried, you had better come to God in prayer and say "As rough as it is right now, Lord, I still want to thank You." Do not let the devil get you to thinking that you do not have anything to thank God for. Please do not ever think that it cannot get any worse. Things can always be worse so thank God for the way things are. Even if you have been evicted, when you do not know where the money is coming from, when your car needs repairs, you still need to say, "God, I thank You that I'm Your child, and because I'm Your child, You promised to hear my prayer. I thank You that I have breath in my body. I thank You that I'm wise enough to pray. I thank You that I haven't killed myself already because I've

No matter what you are going through, you can always tell God, "Thank You."

been through hell." No matter what you're going through, you can always tell God, "Thank You."

God says when you come to Him, He does not just want to hear about how tough it is or how it is not working or how everybody is against you. At some point, God wants to hear you say, "Thank you." He wants to hear it because the more you thank Him, the more you will forget about what you are going through and the more you will count your blessings. You have more working for you than against you.

There is a story about a little boy who told his grandfather that he wanted some Nike shoes. The grandfather said he would get them for him the next day, but the grandmother said, "Don't buy that boy Nikes. He doesn't need those expensive shoes. Take him down to K-mart. He always wants something." The grandfather started thinking, "Maybe I shouldn't buy him those shoes, because if Mama ain't happy, ain't nobody happy." Just as the grandfather was about to doze off to sleep, the boy walked up the stairs, looked into the grandfather's room and said, "Granddad, before I go to bed, all I want to tell

When you start seeking God and speaking to God, and thanking God, He will give you peace in the midst of the storm.

you is I love you." Granddad told the boy, "I'm going to get you two pair of shoes tomorrow."

Sometimes you ought to tell God, "All I want to say is "I love you." I know I have a long way to go. I know I'm not everything I need to be. I know I let you down sometimes. I know I can be critical sometimes. I know I can be moody sometimes, but I do want to let you know that I love you with my whole heart." Paul says *"with thanksgiving let your requests be made known unto God" (Phil. 4:6).*

In verse 7, Paul explains, *"And the peace of God, which passeth all understanding, shall keep your hearts and minds."* In other words, when you start seeking God and speaking to God, and thanking God, He will give you peace in the midst of the storm. Paul is suggesting that God will give you so much peace, people will think you are crazy. You can stand in the unemployment line saying, "God's been good to me." When you have just lost your job you can say, "God closed a window, but He'll open a door." If your husband says, "I want a divorce," you can still praise the Lord anyhow.

Paul continues encouraging the Philippians saying:

> *"Finally, brethren, whatsoever things are true, whatsoever things are honest, whatsoever things are just, whatsoever things are pure, whatsoever things are lovely, whatsoever things are of good report; if there be any virtue, and if there be any praise, think on these things. Those things, which ye have both*

> *learned, and received, and*
> *heard, and seen in me, do: and*
> *the God of peace shall be with*
> *you" (Phil. 4:8–9).*

You have to get away from your negative environment. Sometimes you need to quit watching the news because you get depressed whenever the news comes on. As soon as the news come on you sink into depression.

5. Sling it on God

When a situation arises that tempts you to worry, you have to get rid of it quickly. Get it off of you. When you sling something, even if the other person does not catch it, you are getting rid of it. When you pass something, you have to wait on the other person to grab it, but when you sling something, you are letting it go. First Peter 5:7 says to cast all your cares on him because he cares for you.

God says, "Give Me everything you're worried about. Make a deposit into me." Do you know why God says make a deposit? It is because one day you will need to make a withdrawal. You cannot make a withdrawal, if you have not deposited something into His hands. My brothers Keith, Kevin, Kincaid and I used to sing a song in Vacation Bible School

Life is all about whose hands you put it in.

called "He's Got the Whole World in His Hands." Since He has the whole world in His hands, He can handle whatever you are dealing with.

Do you know what I have discovered? Life is all about whose hands you put it in. A baseball bat in my hands is a dangerous weapon, but in the hands of Barry Bonds, it is a home run champion. A golf club in my hands just means a ball going the wrong way. Golf clubs in Tiger Woods' hands is a Masters championship. A tennis racket in my hand is nothing more than wood and string, but a tennis racket in Venus and Serena Williams' hands means a Wimbledon championship. A slingshot in my hand is just a toy, but in David's hands it took down a giant. Two fish and five loaves in my hands is an appetizer, but in the hands of the Master, they will feed a multitude. Nails in my hands are a painful experience, but nails in the hands of Jesus means victory over death, hell and the grave. Each and everyday He says, "Put it in my hands. Why are you worried? Why are you trying to figure it out? I've already worked it out."

Maybe it has been in your hands and all it produced is bad credit, two divorces and seven bad relationships. Dare to say, "Lord, I'm putting it in Your hands." After Peter says, *"Casting all your cares upon Him for He careth for you,"* he tells us in verse 10, *"But the God of all grace, who hath called us unto his eternal glory by Christ Jesus, after that ye have suffered a while, make you perfect, stablish, strengthen, settle you."* Some people want to be settled, established, strengthened and perfect, but they do not want to suffer. However, God says, "I won't do that until you have suffered a while. I have to allow you to suffer because when you suffer I can make more out of you than I can when everything is going your way." If you are anything like me, you pray a little quicker when you are suffering. If you are like me, you are not late for church when you are suffering.

Suffering gets our attention. It is hard for God to get your attention when you can afford to treat everybody at the restaurant, but when there is more month left than money, you have a way of turning to the Lord praying, "I can't do anything until You come." The good news is that you do not have to worry. Besides, worrying does not make it any better.

There are only two things in life that you should not worry about. The first is the things you cannot control and the second is the things you can. You do not want to worry about things you cannot control because even when you worry about them, you cannot change the outcome.

You also do not want to worry about things you can control. Why? Because if you can control it, you need to quit worrying about it, get up and do something to change it. You cannot do anything about whether an interviewer is going to hire you or not, but you can do something about getting to the interview on time. You cannot do anything about whether someone likes you, but you can do something about being likeable. Either way, worrying is not the solution because it does not change anything. Trusting in God is the key. He can and does change things.

Winning The Battle
ONE ROUND AT A TIME

"Thus saith the Lord unto you, be not afraid nor dismayed by reason of this great multitude; for the battle is not yours, but God's" (II Chronicles 20:15).

In the world of heavyweight boxing, we often think of the classic battles of the world's greatest gladiators. Who could forget the mighty warriors in battle for the coveted title of undisputed heavyweight champion of the world? Forever etched in our memories are the battles of Sonny Liston vs. Cassius Clay, Ali vs. Frazier, Ali vs. Foreman and Holyfield vs. Tyson.

Historically speaking, few great boxing battles were won with a single knock-out punch delivered in a single round. More often than not, the battle was ultimately won painstakingly, methodically and strategically one round at a time. So it is in winning the battle over negative emotions. We must step into the ring and conquer our negative emotions—one round at a time through the Word of God. The key to our victory is in knowing that the battle is not our's, but God's.

At some point, we all step into the ring of negative emotions, but thank God, He allows us to overcome and prevail over every round of bitterness, depression, fear, grief, guilt, hatred, jealousy and worry. When the referee tallies the scorecard round by round, he will pronounce that the battle was fought and the victory won. For we are more than conquerors through Him that loves us.

About The
AUTHOR

— Kerwin B. Lee —

Pastor Kerwin B. Lee was born in Mansfield, Louisiana to the parents of Philip and Thelma Lee. Although born in Louisiana, he was reared and educated in Los Angeles, California. After completing high school, he accepted a basketball scholarship to attend Central Arizona College in Colledge, Arizona, where he graduated with an Associate of Arts degree in General Education.

He furthered his education and basketball college career by attending the University of Alaska-Fairbanks, where he obtained his bachelor's begree in elementary education.

It was while in Alaska that he heard and accepted his call to preach and to prepare for full-time ministry. Being obedient to the call, he enrolled in the Interdenominational Theological Center (ITC) in Atlanta, Georgia, where he earned a Master of Divinity degree in Christian Education. He also received a Doctor of Divinity degree from St. Thomas Christian College in Jacksonville, Florida.

Pastor Lee's Christian service and ministerial impact has been extremely diverse. He has served as a:

- Counselor with the Billy Graham Crusade
- Student pastor in Kingston, Jamaica
- Adjunct professor at Luther Rice Seminary in Atlanta
- Staff member for Young Life, a para-church organization

He is currently senior pastor of the Berean Christian Church in Stone Mountain, Georgia. He is also the founder and president of A Word for the Times Ministries.

He is happily married to his lovely wife, Yolanda. They are the proud parents of two dynamic boys, Kerwin II and Kernard.

Pastor Kerwin B. Lee is rapidly becoming an influential force in the Christian community throughout the United States. He is a widely sought speaker at revivals, conferences, seminars, workshops and retreats. You may contact Kerwin B. Lee at:

Berean Christian Church
2201 Young Road
Stone Mountain, Georgia 30088
www.bereanchristianchurch.org
Office: (770) 593 - 4421
   Fax: (770) 593 - 9124